cucina
rom
ana
sara manuelli

cucina romana

sara manuelli

Interlink Books

An imprint of Interlink Publishing Group, Inc.
Northampton, Massachusetts

First published in 2005 by

INTERLINK BOOKS

An imprint of Interlink Publishing Group, Inc.

46 Crosby Street, Northampton, Massachusetts 01060

www.interlinkbooks.com

Library of Congress Cataloging-in-Publication Data available

ISBN 1-56656-625-8 (paperback)

Publishing Director: Lorraine Dickey
Commissioning Editor: Katey Day
Design: Lucy Gowans
Photography: Lisa Linder
Production Manager: Angela Couchman

Printed and bound in China

To request our complete 40-page full-color catalog, please call us toll
free at 1-800-238-LINK, visit our website at www.interlinkbooks.com,
or send us an email: info@interlinkbooks.com.

All recipes serve 4 unless otherwise stated.

Roman cuisine is the ultimate comfort food. Delicious and simple to prepare, it has enjoyed a reputation among foodies since the days of the Roman emperors. Yet while the recipes of neighboring Tuscany are well known to the international public, the culinary delights of Rome and surrounding areas have still to be fully discovered.

Since the times of Lucullian, then centuries later of papal banquets, food has been the center of social life. In Petronius' Satyricon, the Trimalchio feast chapter presents us with a detailed and amusing account of a decadent, lengthy banquet set during Nero's empire in which only the appetizers consisted of "… dormice seasoned with honey and poppyseed. There were sausages, too, smoking hot on a silver grill, and underneath (to imitate coals) Syrian plums and pomegranate seeds."

As early as AD 60, Apicius was writing *De re Coquinaria*, one of the oldest cookbooks ever found, and a mine of information on ancient Roman cuisine. Apicius was known for his hedonistic lifestyle and for serving extravagant dishes such as flamingo and nightingale tongues, camel heels, roasted ostrich, and stuffed sterile sow's womb. He was also credited by Pliny with forcefeeding geese to enlarge their livers. This would indicate that the origins of foie gras are Italian instead of French. Apicius chronicles the city's obsession with pasta, then known as *laganum*, arguably the very first type of lasagne. He writes how it was served with *garum*, the fermented fish paste, or with a dressing of honey and pepper.

Today Roman cuisine is much simpler, as over the centuries elements of the peasant *cucina povera* (poor cuisine) have taken over from the richer and spicier diet of the emperors and popes. The ancient Roman influence is still there, with the consumption of staples such as pizza, breads, anchovies, and pork firmly entrenched in every Roman's genetic make-up. Above all, however, this is a cuisine born from daily necessity which uses gutsy, simple ingredients such as vine-ripened tomatoes, legumes, pancetta, lamb, chicory, artichokes, and fresh egg pasta.

Regardless of our globalized, frenetic times, Romans still relish meal times as an occasion for conviviality, gossip, and pleasure, and like nothing better than spending a long evening eating in the

many open air *trattorie* (family-run restaurants). An ancient proverb states, "At the table one never grows old," and it is widely known that Romans hate solitude and cannot think of anything better than eating in large numbers, elbow to elbow, in front of steaming typical dishes.

Three influences define Roman cuisine. The first one stems from the city's Jewish community, whose diaspora is the oldest in Europe. Although Roman-Jewish cuisine has evolved over the centuries, perhaps the most significant era was the period from the 1500s to the 1800s, when the Jews were confined within the four gates of the Ghetto during the day. Being sealed off from outside influences, they relied on whatever food was available. This period gave rise to the *friggitori*, street vendors who battered and fried whatever ingredients were readily on hand, creating delicious, cheap street food. The quintessential dishes of Roman-Jewish cooking came straight out of this tradition: *carciofi alla giudia* (Jewish-style artichokes), *filetti di baccalà* (salt cod filets) and fried zucchini flowers stuffed with anchovies and mozzarella. Roman-Jewish cuisine follows the traditional religious calendar of festivities, as well as the numerous strict dietary rules. The Jewish Ghetto, full of friendly restaurants, is still home to some sublime examples of the *cucina ebraico romanesca*, although many of the recipes have been so comprehensively assimilated into Roman cuisine that it is sometimes difficult to distinguish between the two.

The second influence is the Lazio region around Rome, in particular Ciociaria, arguably the home of *spaghetti alla carbonara* (coalminer-style spaghetti with eggs and pancetta) and of *amatriciana* pasta. Such is the pride towards one's produce that most Lazio towns even have *sagras* (festivals) entirely devoted to a special ingredient or dish. Amatrice has an annual sagra for *bucatini all'amatriciana*, Ladispoli features an artichoke sagra, Marino a grape one and Roccantica *la sagra del frittello* (cauliflower tops battered and deep-fried in the regional dark-green Sabine olive oil). The plain of Fondi produces artichokes, black olives, and buffalo mozzarella, while the Castelli Romani are the hills from where the blond, honey-scented Frascati wine comes.

The third influence is the cuisine of the slaughterhouse based in the old quarter of Testaccio, invented by those who worked there and were often paid with leftover scraps of offal. For those who can bear the thought, these are definitely recipes to try at least, as the taste is often delicate and the condiments kept simple. Creamy baby milk-fed veal intestines are teamed with juicy tomato rigatoni, oxtail is braised for hours in dark cocoa until it reaches its trademark condensed flavor, and *trippa alla romana* (tripe) is flavored with spearmint and strong pecorino cheese. The recipes that originate from Testaccio summarize the Romans' love affair with meat.

Finally one must remember the Catholic rule of *giorni cadenzati*, which states the canonical calendar for lean days such as Tuesdays, Fridays, Christmas Eve, and Lent. This is when meat was forbidden, hence the hefty consumption of fish as an alternative. This rhythmic order to meals has influenced many Romans' eating patterns, and still today restaurants serve only a certain type of meal on a prescribed day, such as gnocchi on a Thursday or lamb with potatoes on a Sunday.

This book is a journey into Roman cuisine via a gastronomic tour of its stores and restaurants, producers and chefs, traditions and innovations. Like a travelogue, it provides an itinerary into different Roman districts, each representing a particular approach to food which is encapsulated by the recipes. Importantly, it celebrates the rise of what was once dismissed as *cucina burina*, or the cuisine of *burini*, simple country folk who would come to Rome to sell butter. This cooking tradition may for a long time have been considered unsophisticated, but this has now changed. Today many Lazio restaurants are a breeding ground for talented chefs who exploit the advantage of top-notch local produce to create a cuisine that is fast gaining rewards in the best food guides.

The book looks at the past, but it is mostly interested in the present. It looks at how Romans and Lazio restaurateurs are busy reinventing tradition with a renewed focus on food production, whether organic or by methods which have been certified as "authentic" by associations such as the Italian Slow Food movement. Thanks to this new attitude we can now talk of a producers' renaissance, one where small batch farmers, winegrowers, and olive-oil makers of the Lazio region are discovering how essential it is to preserve ancient skills, as well as the individuality of their product. Added to this is the recent rise of the knowledgeable customer who is increasingly demanding quality rather than quantity, and who appreciates the fruits of hard labor and is ready to pay the price for them. A new food movement has been born, and nowhere seems more relevant to taste it than in Rome today.

campo dei fiori

Campo dei Fiori

If you walk up Via dei Cappellari, a winding alley of a street, named after the hat makers who had workshops here in medieval times, you reach a large open, bustling square. Campo dei Fiori – literally, "field of flowers" – was a select residential district in the sixteenth century (the aristocratic Orsini family had a palace here), as well as the center of the hotel trade. Framed by pastel-hued palazzi, recently restored in Pompeiian reds, topaz blues, and terracotta oranges, it is the only square in Rome without a church, no mean feat in such a Catholic city. Indeed, the square's centerpiece is a statue of Giordano Bruno, a heretic burned at the stake in 1600, as if to remind us that the square was frequently used as a place for execution.

Today, Campo dei Fiori is a tourist destination and home to one of the oldest fruit, vegetable, and flower markets in Rome. The square constantly transforms itself throughout the day. At dawn, carts rattle on the cobblestones on their way to the stalls, laden with tightly packed wooden crates of fruit and vegetables. Later it fills with fruit and vegetable sellers and regular local shoppers, patiently mingling with spellbound tourists. The noise levels rapidly rise, as shouting, singing, joking, and teasing are all part of a Roman seller's repertoire. Crates of sun-blessed zucchini, crispy *puntarelle* salad, and ripe purple artichokes from Ladispoli are sold alongside fresh cut flowers and fish from the nearby sea port of Fiumicino. Around midday, the frenzy subsides slightly, as most shoppers return home and the trattorie around the square start putting out tables and chairs to entice punters. At about 2 pm the stalls pack up, the sellers chatting and laughing as they manage to pile huge amounts of empty wooden boxes onto precariously small Ape scooters. Tramps and stray dogs pick at the bruised melons and squashed tomatoes, before the sweepers clean up and disinfect the square. A Roman minstrel, complete with mandolin and a repertoire of Roman songs, does the rounds of the tables at the trattorie. What follows is a peaceful period during which the square's cobblestones glisten squeaky clean, and mothers with children enjoy the pedestrian area for an afternoon *passeggiata*.

Towards six in the evening, as people finish work and spill out on the streets, the local wine shop, La Vineria, run by the Reggio family, becomes the hotspot of the square. Once the haunt of alcoholic bohemians such as Beat poet Gregory Corso, today La Vineria is where the beautiful, tanned Roman youth hang out with a chilled glass of Prosecco to gossip. Later still into the night, the square fills to its capacity, with people sitting

Opposite: The fruit and vegetable market at Campo dei Fiori, one of the oldest in Rome, is the center of neighborhood life. Here stall vendors from the Lazio countryside mix with family run butcher shops and bakeries.

Food lovers' address book

Il Fiorentino (butchery)
Piazza Campo dei Fiori 17/18
tel +39 06 68801296

Roscioli (wine and deli shop)
Via dei Giubbonari 21/22
tel +39 06 6875287

Il Forno di Campo dei Fiori
(bakery)
Campo dei Fiori 22
tel +39 06 68806662

Il Forno (delicatessen)
Vicolo del Gallo 14

Antica Norcineria Viola
(pork butchery)
Campo dei Fiori 43
tel +39 06 68806114

Marco Roscioli (bakery)
Via dei Chiavari 34
tel +39 06 6864045

Il Filettaro di Santa Barbara
(for fried salt cod)
Largo dei Librari 88
tel +39 06 6864018

on the empty flower stalls, strolling to and fro, and generally waiting for something to happen.

Remnants of old Roman life are still visible. Until 20 years ago, a cart horse would carry piles of artichokes to the market, then feast itself on the discarded leaves at the end of the day. Women still carry flowers balanced on their head garb, like the old Roman peasants in the nineteenth century. The knife sharpener appears once a month on his bicycle, an ingeniously conceived system that sharpens knives thanks to the speed of his pedaling. Housewives run towards him with rusty kitchen utensils, but the rationale behind his appearances is anybody's guess.

You cannot wander for long in the Campo without smelling a raft of freshly baked bread and yearning for a piece of pizza from Il Forno, the bakery that is pretty much the heart of the square. At every hour of the day Il Forno churns out fragrant rosettes, the Roman five-diamond shaped buns; olive bread; crusty *pane casereccio*; sweet *panini all'olio*, baked in olive oil; and its deliciously warm *pizza rossa* with tomato and *pizza bianca*, seasoned only with coarse sea salt. A few years ago, the owner Mario capitalized on Il Forno's baking skills, excellent produce, and affectionate clientele, and opened another bakery next door – specializing in more delicatessen-like products, such as pizza with zucchini flowers and mozzarella, or calzoni stuffed with chard and black olives. During carnival, Il Forno bakes sugar-coated frappe and castagnole, sweet fritters that everyone gorges themselves on right up until the frenzy of Mardi Gras. In the winter, out comes the dark castagnaccio, a chestnut-flour cake peppered with pine nuts, raisins, and a few sprigs of rosemary.

Further down in the square is the Norcineria Viola, which sells *guanciale* (cured pork jowl), a staple of Roman dishes such as *spaghetti alla carbonara*. This family-run institution has been on the square since 1880 and is today managed by three brothers and a cousin. Yet, as in all urban centers, things are changing fast on Rome's gastronomic map, and the Viola clan bemoans the lack of interest on the part of the new generation in inheriting the business. Like all pork butchers in Rome, they came originally from Norcia in the Umbria region, hence the name *norcini*. Wild boars and pigs roamed this land full of forests, and the norcini were traditionally seasonal workers who, when not butchering, would make straw hats. At the beginning of the twentieth century, many norcini left their hometown to find work and spread their skills across Italy. The norcini are masters at all treatments of all types of meat, but it is with pork that they excel. Norcineria Viola makes wild boar sausages, cures succulent hams, presses pork leftovers into a monumental composition called *schiacciata o coppa romana* (seasoned with fennel or lemon or orange zest), smokes bacon and spices guanciale with coarse salt and pepper. One of the few "true" Roman products on sale is *le coppiette*, strips of dried pork meat considered an aphrodisiac because of their heavy chili seasoning. For Easter, the Norcineria Viola sells *corallina salame*, traditionally eaten in Rome with *la torta pasqualina* (Easter cake). Most of the produce is cut and prepared in the back rooms of the store and still sent up to Norcia, where it is cured in the open air of the Sibillini hills. Viola admits that while the artistry in preparing pork has managed to maintain itself thanks to the passing down through the generations, the quality of pork itself has over the years somehow lost its excellence. Gone are the pork "shepherds" – usually children or older men – who would feed the pig with household scraps and take him into the woods to eat acorns. Large batch farming has led to a blandness in the meat, and it is difficult to farm organic pigs without heavily affecting the retail price, something Viola believes would not go down very well among his customers.

A positive story of gastronomic reinvention comes from Roscioli, run by a family of bakers by tradition who still own four bakeries around Rome (and are related to Mario the baker on Campo dei Fiori). Down the Giubbonari road, so called because it is where the makers of *giubbe* (jackets) used to have their workshops, is the Roscioli *alimentari*, which sells a wide selection of top-class Italian cheeses, salami, and wines, and is fast becoming a firm favorite among food editors worldwide. At the back, the store doubles up as a small restaurant/*enoteca* (wine bar) serving a light menu and an excellent selection of wines by the glass.

Roscioli is the brainchild of the Roscioli brothers – Alessandro on the wines and Pierluigi on front of house and produce – who, having worked since they were 11 in their parent's nearby bakery, know a thing or two about customer service. Pierluigi says it was an early visit to Dean and Deluca in New York that inspired him to create a food store which would balance tradition and innovation. It is the brothers' entrepreneurial approach and their constant attention towards quality, however, that have made Roscioli a truly Roman success. On the counter are beautifully stacked goodies such as the *canestrato* cheese, produced near Latina and made from sheep's and goat's milk; hams from the nearby Lazio town of Amatrice; cojoni di mulo (literally "mule's bullocks"), a type of salami stuffed with small specks of lard; and huge shapes of *caciocchiato*, a cheese which the Roscioli buy in the Irpinia region, then season in their own caves in Le Marche for another four months. Roscioli stocks most of Italy's established wine producers, as well as a varied selection of balsamic vinegars and extra-virgin olive oils. Customers can sample everything before buying and are often advised about possible wine combinations with the food they buy. Pierluigi has plenty of interesting catering ideas for the future, which will no doubt be successful as both brothers are hard workers, passionate, and always provide a courteous service.

Spaghetti alla carbonara
Coal-miner's spaghetti

Although on Campo dei Fiori there is a restaurant called La Carbonara, it is fair to say that this incredibly simple dish can be found well executed in most Roman restaurants. As always, the secret is in the ingredients and, if you are in the area, you can buy *guanciale* from the Norcineria Viola. When it comes to *carbonara*, there are two different stories of genesis. Some say that it was a dish introduced at the time of the American allies occupation of Rome during World War II because it combines bacon and eggs, staples of an American breakfast, with pasta. The other plays on the etymological origin of the dish's name, a gutsy dish for coal-miners, who were traditionally nomadic and would carry with them long-lasting ingredients such as dried pasta, guanciale, pecorino cheese, and chickens for fresh eggs.

1 lb spaghetti
4 strips guanciale or pancetta
olive oil
3 eggs, beaten
freshly grated pecorino or Parmesan cheese
freshly ground black pepper

Bring a large pan of salted water to the boil; when ready, immerse the spaghetti. At the same time, slowly fry the guanciale in a large frying pan or skillet with a little olive oil until crunchy. Remove from the pan and set aside, and keep the pan sitting over a very low heat. Just before the spaghetti is cooked, scoop out some of the boiling water – you can use it later to moisten the pasta. When the spaghetti is al dente, drain quickly and place in the warm frying pan. Pour in the eggs, bacon and some of the reserved boiling water. Stir quickly until you reach your preferred consistency – I like my eggs quite cooked, but some people serve carbonara sauce very runny.

Remove from the heat and put in a warmed serving bowl. Grind plenty of pepper over the spaghetti, and sprinkle a good dose of pecorino over the top. Serve immediately – lukewarm pasta defies the point.

Paja e fieno, funghi e piselli
Pasta with mushrooms and peas

This is an incredibly easy and satisfying dish to make. One of the best *paja e fieno* (literally "hay and straw") can be found in Osteria Romanesca on Campo dei Fiori, an unassuming trattoria that is always packed. Paja e fieno is an egg pasta so named because of its trademark yellow and green color, achieved with the use of a little spinach in the pasta dough. It works well with subtle rich and creamy sauces.

1 red onion, sliced
olive oil
7 oz (1 1/2 cups) shelled green peas, fresh or frozen
8 oz button mushrooms
1 lb fresh paja e fieno or tagliatelle egg pasta
1 cup light cream
freshly grated Parmesan cheese
a few basil leaves

Bring a large pan of salted water to the boil. In the meantime, gently fry the red onion in a little olive oil until just softened, then add the peas and mushrooms, and cook for about 10 minutes. If the vegetables seem dry, add just a little bit of water. Pour in the cream and allow the mixture to simmer slowly over a very low heat for a minute.

Pour the pasta into the boiling water – it should not take more than a couple of minutes to cook. Set some of the cooking water aside for the final stage, then drain the pasta and toss it into the pan with the mushroom mixture. If it needs moisture, add a little of the reserved pasta water. Serve with plenty of Parmesan and a few basil leaves as garnish.

Opposite: Guanciale

Zuppa di fave, patate, funghi e pecorino romano
Fava bean, potato, oyster mushroom, and pecorino soup

This recipe comes from the young chef at Roscioli, Paolo Dalicandro, who carefully mixes traditional Roman ingredients such as fava beans and pecorino cheese with more inventive cooking procedures. In his spare time, Paolo plays the pipes in the only Roman Celtic band, but luckily he still has time to concoct great dishes.

1 celery stalk, chopped
1 carrot, chopped
1 small white onion, sliced
olive oil
2 new potatoes (such as Charlotte), diced
10 oz (2 cups) shelled fava beans or 2 lb fava beans in their pods
8 oz oyster mushrooms
2 tablespoons vegetable stock
freshly shaved pecorino or Parmesan cheese (optional)
crusty bread, broken into chunks and toasted (optional)

Sauté the celery, carrot, and onion in a little olive oil until the onion has softened. Remove from the pan with a slotted spoon, but do not discard the cooking juices. Once cool, purée in a liquidizer or food processor, or push through a sieve.

Meanwhile parboil the potato in a pan of salted water. Blanch the fava beans, then sauté in the same pan as the carrot mixture for about 5 minutes to give them flavor.

Slightly grill the mushrooms under a moderately hot preheated broiler then place in a large pan with the celery purée, fava beans, and potato. Pour in at least 61/3 cups water. Add the vegetable stock and cook the soup over a low heat for about 30–40 minutes, adding more water if necessary.

Serve the soup in bowls with pecorino shavings and toasted chunks of crusty bread sprinkled over the top if you wish.

Insalata di puntarelle con alici
Puntarelle salad with an anchovy dressing

You cannot get a more Roman ingredient than *puntarelle*, a type of bitter Catalonian chicory the stalks of which are cut into fine, white, curly strips. Romans consider puntarelle a delicacy, but often buy it pre-prepared as it requires a lengthy preparation time. In Campo dei Fiori, deft stall-holders swiftly cut the stalks into long slivers by pushing them through wire mesh, then place them in cold water tubs to curl them, but you could easily do it at home with a small, sharp knife. The way to temper the bitterness of the stalks is to toss them with an anchovy dressing, lots of lemon juice, and oil. Unfortunately, puntarelle is quite difficult to find outside Rome, although some Italian delicatessens do import it – a common substitute for this salad is celery.

7 oz puntarelle or 6 large celery stalks, cut into fine slivers (discard all the hard, stringy bits)

For the anchovy dressing
5 desalted anchovy filets, finely chopped, or 2 teaspoons anchovy paste
good-quality extra-virgin olive oil
2 garlic cloves, chopped
good pinch of sea salt

Cut the puntarelle into fine slivers, discarding all the hard stringy bits. Put the slivers in a bowl of chilled water for 5-10 minutes until they curl. Drain and pat dry thoroughly.

To make the dressing, combine all the ingredients and warm gently over a low heat. Place the puntarelle in a serving bowl, toss the warm dressing through the salad and serve immediately.

Cappuccino di ricotta

Ricotta cheese cappuccino

Fresh sheep's milk ricotta is one of the few Roman cheeses that is still produced by farmers in the neighboring countryside and transported daily to the city, where it should ideally consumed within two days. Its delicate flavor and malleable consistency mean it can be eaten simply with a tiny sprinkling of sugar or folded in cakes and *crostate* (tarts). This sweet treat comes from Paolo at Roscioli, and it combines his love for the Roman cheese and coffee. It features a staple of Italian pâtisseries, the nutty chocolate cookies called *brutti ma buoni* ("ugly but good"), but any cookies with chocolate and nuts will do.

4 hard chocolate and nut cookies, brutti ma buoni if possible
10 oz fresh ricotta
1 teaspoon ground coffee beans
scant 1/2 cup freshly brewed coffee
scant 1/2 cup whipping cream, whipped
1/2 cup superfine sugar, plus 2 tablespoons extra for caramel

Process or crush the cookies into coarse crumbs, then mix together all the ingredients in a bowl, except the extra sugar. Divide the mixture into six dessert or parfait glasses, and place in the refrigerator for a couple of hours to rest.

To make the caramel for decoration, heat the sugar with a little water, stirring continuously, until a thick, dark caramel is formed, then quickly drizzle a few streaks of caramel onto a sheet of baking parchment. When the caramel has dried and set, gently peel off the paper and break into sections that you can use to decorate the top of the dessert.

La pizza bianca

Roman-style white pizza

Whether you like it crunchy or chewy, Roman *pizza bianca* is the most satisfying of street snacks. Unlike the Neapolitan one, Roman pizza is like a flat bread and comes either *bianca* (white) – ever so slightly burnt at the edges, with a good sprinkling of coarse sea salt – or *rossa* (red) – with a very thin layer of tomato sauce. Bakers such as Il Forno and Roscioli sell it sliced, cut in two, and wrapped in dark brown paper to absorb the olive oil, while specialized *pizzerie al taglio* offer every topping under the earth, from potatoes and rosemary to artichokes and ham. This recipe comes from Roscioli's oven.

Serves 8

7 1/2 cups Italian white flour (type 0.020.0)
1/3 oz fresh live yeast or 1/4 oz packet easy-blend dried yeast
2 teaspoons granulated sugar
3 cups warm water
extra-virgin olive oil
about 2 teaspoons coarse sea salt

Mix the flour in a large bowl with the salt, yeast, sugar, and the water, adding more flour or water if necessary, to make a firm dough. Knead for at least 10 minutes until it forms a shiny, sticky ball. Allow to rest for at least 2 hours at room temperature.

When the dough has doubled in size, punch it down. Sprinkle with flour and cut into four. Knead each piece for about a minute until slightly sticky. Use your fist to press into loaf shapes. Brush the tops with plenty of olive oil and sprinkle with sea salt. Leave to rise for another hour. The dough will soak up all the oil and salt, which determines the crispiness of the pizza.

Place the loaves on a flat surface dusted with flour. Knead each one into a 10-inch circle about 3/4-inch thick. The more you work your fingertips into the dough, the flatter the pizza will be. Transfer to a baking sheet dusted with flour. Bake in a preheated oven at 475°–500°F for 12–15 minutes until golden. Serve warm.

piazza nav ona

Piazza Navona

This landmark square in the historical center of Rome is called "Navona" because of its long, shiplike shape. Fittingly it has been, in its past, the scene of many re-enacted water battles. According to local myth, it was here that the two sculptors Borromini and Bernini battled out their fierce rivalry, Borromini building the baroque Saint Agnes church and Bernini responding with the central Fountain of the Four Rivers. The legend relates to the character representing the river Nile, who has his face covered so as not to see the facade of Saint Agnes, while the river Plate character raises his hand as if to prevent the church from falling.

Now a pedestrian area, Piazza Navona is a focal point for tourists, who wander among the stall vendors selling watercolors and miniatures of the baroque architecture. In December, Piazza Navona sheds its picture-postcard image to become the site of the Christmas fair. For six weeks, a carousel, a life-sized crib, and stalls selling cheap toys and kaleidoscopic candies enthral hordes of Italian children.

The area is largely known for beautiful and pricey apartments, rather than good-quality restaurants and food stores. The only café of note is Tre Scalini on the square, an old establishment famous thanks to its chocolate *tartufo*, a truffle-shaped ice cream served with a generous dose of whipped cream. If one looks behind the tourist traps and tacky surface, however, gems can still be found. Just off the square, down Arco della Pace, the tiny market of Piazza del Fico survives – merely four vegetable stalls, but still serving the original community. In Via del Governo Vecchio is Baffetto, one of the oldest pizzerias of the neighborhood, and one of the few Roman establishments left where it is still possible to have a hearty meal for about 12 euros. Speed is the key at this establishment, as waiters whiz around tables balancing six or seven plates in their hands, and the *pizzaioli* knead, flip, and shove the pizzas in the large wood-fired oven.

Baffetto's pizzas are legendary, their flat, crusty base totally different from the Neapolitan type. Toppings are reassuringly simple: *marinara*, so called because the tomato is flavored with anchovies; *funghi*, with a multitude of thinly sliced mushrooms; and *capricciosa* – literally meaning "capricious" – overflowing with artichokes, ham, and eggs. Customers arrive early to avoid the long lines, gobble up the pizzas and depart, allowing a second sitting to take place. The owner, Baffetto, named for his signature moustache, oversees the operations and makes sure that the crowds are always content and entertained. The proof of his hospitality skills lies in the multitude

Opposite: The Fountain of the Four Rivers in Piazza Navona. According to the myth, the Baroque sculptor Bernini built the fountain to obscure the nearby church of Saint Agnes designed by rival architect Borromini.

of photographs that plaster the walls of him posing with Italian celebrities.

Further up the road, where Via del Governo Vecchio becomes Via dei Banchi Nuovi, is Alfredo e Ada. Trying to find a place at this eight-table restaurant needs real patience and determination, but once inside you are rewarded by being treated as part of the family. Ada Ricciutelli has been running this place since 1945, and every day, from the premises of a cramped kitchenette, she cooks lunch and dinner. Just as in a trattoria of the past, customers are given a pitcher of wine and another of water, and told about the three or four dishes available that day. Always on the menu is Ada's speciality, veal *spezzatino* (stew) with peas, and other Roman classics such as egg frittata, or tripe with tomato sauce. The service here is informal, and customers from different tables often share snippets of conversation as in a large communal canteen.

On the other side of the street is a completely different type of establishment, L'Altro Mastai restaurant, which serves top innovative Italian fare. L'Altro Mastai is the brainchild of young chef Fabio Baldessarre who has worked with Heinz Beck, the Michelin star chef at the Hilton restaurant La Pergola in Rome. Fabio previously worked at Raymond Blanc's Les Quatre Saisons in Summertown, Oxford. To dine at L'Altro Mastai is to take a journey into the wide spectrum of Italian flavors. A tender swordfish filet is teamed up with a puree of cauliflower and oranges, and served with marinated sea bass eggs; spaghetti is tossed with a moist sauce of wild asparagus and prawns. Although Fabio's cooking is far too worldly to be pinned down to a regional tradition, he is incredibly caring about using only local and seasonal produce, which is at the core of his well-executed dishes. L'Altro Mastai is high priced, and the reward is a range of subtle dishes and a formal service among the highest quality in Rome. Next door to the restaurant is Fabio's successful wine bar, Il Bicchiere di Mastai, which serves a wide selection of Italian labels, as well as light meals. On Thursdays, wine producers from Lazio and other Italian regions come here to extol the virtue of their wines in tasting events which have fast become the local area's hot meeting point.

Supplì di riso al telefono
Telephone-style rice croquettes

Endless discussions will take place at pizzeria tables as to why *supplì* (rice croquettes) are called "*al telefono*" – telephone style. The most reasonable answer is that when you bite into the melted mozzarella cheese the stringy bits are a somewhat like a telephone cord. Supplì are a great recycling vehicle and can be made with cheap ingredients such as leftover rice, then stuffed with meat, fresh green peas, or tiny bits of ham.

Makes 10–12 croquettes

2 cups Arborio or Carnaroli rice
2 tomatoes, chopped
olive oil
1 tablespoon shelled green peas, fresh or frozen
2 slices prosciutto cotto or other cured ham, finely shredded
1 fresh mozzarella cheese, about 4 oz
1 egg, beaten
6 tablespoons dry breadcrumbs

Cook the rice using the risotto recipe on page 30, leaving out the fava beans and using water in place of the vegetable stock.

Gently fry the tomato in a little olive oil until the pulp reaches the consistency of a sauce. Blanch the peas quickly in hot water, then add to the rice with the tomato and prosciutto, and stir well. Spoon the rice mixture out of the pan and spread over a clean, cold work surface to cool.

With your hands, scoop a handful of rice mixture and roll it into an oval shape about the size of a squashed golf ball – you should end up with 10–12 supplì. Poke a hole in the middle with your index finger, and stick a piece of the mozzarella inside. Repeat the operation until you have used up all the rice.

One by one, dunk the supplì in the beaten egg, then coat with the breadcrumbs. Heat a pan with plenty of olive oil. Gently add one supplì at a time, cooking until crisp and golden. Remove from the pan and drain on absorbent kitchen paper. Eat warm or cold.

Gnocchi alla romana
Roman-style gnocchi

Roman-style gnocchi are made with semolina and baked in the oven with a topping of butter, tomato, and Parmesan cheese. This version of gnocchi is more delicate than the traditional potato ones and probably more authentic, as semolina flour was used in ancient Roman times – unlike the potato, which was introduced only after the discovery of the Americas. Over the years, potato gnocchi have become the city's favorite, and restaurants serving the semolina version have become fewer. It is, however, an incredibly easy dish to cook at home.

4 1/4 cups milk
1 7/8 cups semolina flour
7 tablespoons unsalted butter
freshly grated Parmesan cheese
1 egg yolk, beaten
13 oz canned plum tomatoes
olive oil

Heat the milk in a pan and, when it reaches boiling point, sprinkle in the semolina flour, stirring constantly with a wooden spoon to avoid any lumps. Lower the heat and keep stirring for 10 minutes, until the consistency of the mixture is very stiff. Remove the pan from the heat and add half of the butter, a bit of Parmesan and the egg yolk. Mix all the ingredients well. Spread the semolina mixture on a slightly damp work surface or a damp large flat plate, and allow to cool for at least 1 hour.

Cook the plum tomatoes for 10 minutes with a little bit of olive oil in a small pan.

Grease a large baking dish with butter. Cut 2 in rounds from the semolina mixture using a cookie cutter or a water glass. Arrange the gnocchi in the baking dish, overlapping them partially. Cover with the tomato sauce, chunks of the remaining butter and a good sprinkle of Parmesan. Bake in a preheated oven at 425°F for 15–20 minutes, until brown. Serve warm topped with extra Parmesan.

Merluzzo marinato su carpaccio tiepido di pomodori
Marinated cod on a bed of warm sliced tomatoes

Although the coast around Rome was always an abundant source of fish, the pick of the day went to those who could afford it, traditionally the bishops and higher echelons of ecclesiastical society.

Catholic rules state that on Fridays one should eat *magro* (lean food), of either fish or chicken, but humble Romans who could not afford fresh fish were forced out of necessity to use cheaper alternatives. This explains the popularity of *baccalà* (salt cod) and *stoccafisso* (dried cod), especially among those housewives who pride themselves in transforming a relatively cheap fish into a delicious meal.

Still today, baccalà can be found soaking in trays in most Roman groceries stores, and I recommend buying it in this guise. Alternatively you can buy it dried and soak it yourself for 48 hours, to dilute the salty flavor. The classic deep-fried baccalà so loved by the Romans is the closest the cuisine comes to English fish and chips, something that may be explained by the Jewish origin of both dishes.

Other ways of eating salt cod are *guazzetto* (in a sauce), *alla trasteverina* (floured strips of fish with capers) and *agrodolce* (a sweet–sour style). As always with any classic dish, everyone has a particular variation of it. And I include this one from Fabio Baldessare, the young, talented chef behind L'Altro

Mastai restaurant, which actually uses fresh cod – although it also works wonders with salt cod.

2 1/4 lb whole fresh cod or desalted salt cod
grated zest of 1 lemon
grated zest of 1 orange
a few sprigs of fresh thyme
olive oil for cooking
4 1/2 lb large medium-ripe tomatoes
extra-virgin olive oil
handful of basil leaves, cut into fine strips
7 oz pitted black olives, chopped
5 oz capers
salt and freshly ground black pepper

Marinate the cod in a bowl with the lemon and orange zest, a pinch of salt (only if you are using fresh cod) and the thyme for 2 hours. Filet the marinated fish with a large serrated knife, then heat a large frying pan with plenty of olive oil. Brown the cod filets quickly on both sides, then remove from the pan.

Meanwhile slice the tomatoes and arrange them on a platter, dressing them with some extra-virgin olive oil, salt and pepper, and the basil leaves. Place the warm cod filet on the tomatoes with a sprinkling of chopped olives and capers, and serve immediately.

Carciofi alla romana
Roman-style artichokes

To achieve true perfection, one should have at one's disposal the artichoke *romanesco*, a species of large globe artichoke found in the stretch of land between Rome and the port town of Civitavecchia. It is a particular favorite in the seaside resort of Ladispoli, which even has a *sagra* (festival) in honor of the artichoke. One can settle for the smaller, more common variety – there will just be less of it to eat. Artichokes form the basis of much Roman cuisine, and you will find them deep-fried Jewish-style, tossed in a pasta sauce with grouper, or battered as snacks. Whichever way you cook it, the clue to a tender artichoke is how you prepare it. Most Roman housewives are particularly adept at the skill, but nowadays many shops serve ready-cleaned artichokes.

4 large globe artichokes
juice of 1 lemon
bunch of mint or flat-leaf parsley, finely chopped
2 garlic cloves, finely chopped
olive oil
salt

Take one of the artichokes and start peeling the leaves off with your hands until you reach the whiter and softer leaves. Chop off half the stem, then peel off the hard skin around the remaining half until the stem feels tender. Cut off the top of the artichoke evenly, to get a tidy and compact shape, then submerge in a bowl of water with some lemon juice added to prevent blackening . Prepare the remaining artichokes in the same way.

Remove the artichokes from the bowl and push them top-down against a chopping board so that they spread slightly. Remove any of the hard, wispy heart (or "choke"), and stuff them with the mint and garlic. Place face down in a pan generously covered with oil. Once they are in, fill the pan with water until it reaches halfway up the artichokes. (Some versions advocate cutting the stems and cooking separately.) Cover with a lid and cook over a medium heat for about 40 minutes until tender.

Roman tradition states that these artichokes can eaten hot or cold, but should never be reheated.

Ciambelle al vino

Ring shape cookies

At the end of each meal at Alfredo and Ada's restaurant, out come *le ciambelle al vino*, hard sweet cookies to be dunked in a chilled glass of white wine. A typical speciality of the Frascati area, they are easily found in most Roman bakeries.

Serves 4–6

3 cups all-purpose flour
1/2 cup granulated sugar
pinch of ground cinnamon
6 tablespoons olive oil
6 tablespoons dry white wine

Mix together the flour, sugar, and cinnamon in a bowl. Add the olive oil and wine, combining until the mixture forms into a dough. Place on a floured work surface and knead until the dough has a rubbery consistency. Take a walnut-sized piece of dough and roll it out into a long strip about 4 in long and about 1/2 in thick. Then join the two extremities to form a ring shape. Gently flatten the cookie and place it on a baking tray covered with baking parchment.

Cook all the cookies in a preheated oven at 375°F for about 20 minutes until golden. Cool before serving.

Risotto alle fave

Risotto with fava beans

When the sweet, buttery fava beans start appearing in the markets of Rome, it is a sign that springtime has arrived. Romans eat them raw, plucked from their pods, with small chunks of salty, crumbling pecorino romano cheese. Chef Fabio Baldessare's risotto with fava beans is a nod towards both Roman produce and Northern Italy's tradition for rice recipes.

3 1/2 oz (5/8 cup) shelled fava beans
1 onion, chopped
a few sprigs of rosemary
7 tablespoons unsalted butter
a little olive oil
2 1/2 cups carnaroli rice
1 1/2 cups dry white wine
8 1/2 cups vegetable stock
3 oz fresh goat's cheese
1 teaspoon white peppercorns
3 tablespoons freshly grated Parmesan cheese
2 teaspoons chopped flat-leaf parsley, plus a few sprigs
salt

Blanch the fava beans in salted, boiling water, then place in a bowl to cool. In a large frying pan, sauté the onion with the rosemary in a bit of the butter and a little olive oil, until the onion is starting to color.

Add the rice and stir through for a few minutes to allow the butter to coat the grains. Pour in the wine and, when evaporated, add a few ladles of the vegetable stock. Cook the rice for about 15 minutes, using enough of the remaining stock to keep it moist. Taste and season with salt if needed.

Add the fava beans and cook briefly, making sure to stir constantly. Remove the pan from the heat and take out the rosemary sprigs. Add the remaining butter, the goat's cheese, Parmesan, and chopped parsley, amalgamating all the ingredients well. Grind a few white peppercorns over the top, add a few parsley sprigs to garnish, and serve in bowls immediately.

campo marzio e piazza di spagna

Campo Marzio e Piazza di Spagna

The area that lies between Campo Marzio, the Pantheon, and Piazza di Spagna is arguably the city's most famous tourist trail, justified by its high concentration of baroque churches, magnificent art, and Renaissance architecture. Such is the beauty of display that it is easy to become nonchalant, but beware because even an unassuming church such as Luigi dei Francesi hides within it three splendid chiaroscuro Caravaggio paintings. Of all the most celebrated Roman landmarks, the one perhaps that most closely resembles ancient Roman life is the Pantheon, built by Hadrian in AD 118 and one of the first temples to be Christianized as Santa Maria ad Martyres in 609. Today it hosts the tombs of Italy's kings and that of the painter Raphael, and is very rarely devoid of tourist crowds admiring its vaulted, hollow rooftop. At Christmas, it hosts a moving candlelit midnight mass, with Gregorian chants resonating up to the dome.

Away from the humming crowds and in the narrow streets are some of the city's best restaurants, cafés, and food stores. Near Santa Maria sopra Minerva is Confetteria Mariondo e Gariglio, a tiny, quaint chocolate store of Piedmontese origin that has been in business in Rome for more than a century, and whose women workers all wear red aprons and dainty white hats. Easter, Christmas, and Saint Valentine's Day are when the store is at its most bustling, with the women busy packing the home-made pralines, chocolate eggs, and truffles in boxes with multicolored ribbons.

Back towards the Pantheon is a Roman institution, the Caffè Sant'Eustachio, reputed to make the best coffee in Rome. The coffee bar takes its name from Eustace, a Roman general who paid his conversion when he was martyred by being burnt alive. Coffee lovers and guided tours from all over world visit the bar reverentially, all intent on sampling its famous *gran caffè*, a strong and creamy coffee slightly sweetened by sugar. Since its invention in 1938, the formula of gran caffè has been kept secret, and the waiters even brew behind a partition so that customers cannot see what they are doing.

A slightly more exclusive pilgrimage food site is the nearby Rosetta restaurant, famed for being the first restaurant in Rome to serve an exclusively fish and seafood menu. According to owner and chef Massimo Riccioli's booklet *Dinner with the Gods* – a fictional account of a romantic dinner between characters such as

Above: As well as being a feat of early engineering, the vaulted, hollow rooftop of the Pantheon is also one of the city's most stunning locations. The entire area is packed with bustling cafes, artisan shops, Baroque churches, and top class restaurants.

Humphrey Bogart and Ingrid Bergman, and the poet Dante and Beatrice – back in the 1920s La Rosetta was the site of a *rosticceria*, a food store where roasted chickens and porchetta ham were sold. When La Rosetta opened in the 1950s under the new management of Massimo's parents, Romana and Carmelo, fish consumption in the city was limited to Tuesdays and Fridays (the traditional lean days) and to simple, poor cuisine dishes such as squid and peas. Soon their passion for Mediterranean fish and cooking talents turned La Rosetta into a favorite haunt of politicians, actors, and businessmen. The legacy of La Rosetta's fish culture can be found today in the many Rome restaurants which serve dishes born here, such as sea bass with orange and salad of arugula and shrimp.

In 1981, Massimo gave up his job as a cameraman to take over the restaurant, focusing on the source of the foods because he believes that the ingredients are the epicenter of any dish. Massimo is a member of the school of thought that the less one does to fish the better, cooking just enough for the flavors to remain intact. He compares his inventive method of cooking to that of a jam session, an act of improvization in which fragrant raw materials are quickly cooked into harmonious combinations. From his delicate tuna tartare to his baby squid in an ink sauce on a bed of mushy peas, or his *strozzapreti* pasta with grouper and sweet eggplant and capers, there is little Massimo cannot turn into an epicurean experience. The high prices mark this restaurant as a cut above the average Roman restaurant, yet the prime choice of fish and other seafood on offer and Massimo's genius justify it completely.

Away from the baroque beauties of Rome's *centro storico* lies the severe-looking rationalist architecture of Piazza Augusto Imperatore, built by Mussolini as a perimeter around the Mausoleum of Augustus, a rather shoddy conical mound of earth in which Augustus and his descendants are said to be buried. Under the arcades that contain the square are several restaurants, but the one that has spearheaded a new type of Roman gastronomy is without doubt Gusto, a large eaterie cum wine bar cum kitchen store started about 10 years ago. Loved by tourists, who probably find the international cuisine and the contemporary décor vaguely familiar and thus reassuring, Gusto has now expanded into the building next door and recently opened yet another restaurant, called Osteria della Frezza. Unlike Gusto, Osteria della Frezza is a clever reinvention of the old-fashioned Roman *hosteria* (the name derives from the word *oste* – the host who would both own the establishment and often be the cook). Not surprisingly, this is a place loved by young Romans, who find the brasserie-style décor and the well-priced meals in tune with the needs for a fun night out. Roman cuisine constitutes the core of the menu, but Italian regional dishes are also available. La Frezza's main attraction, however, is its cheese room, a see-through glass box built inside the eating area which has more than 200 types of French and Italian cheese on view. All are kept at a rigorous temperatures of 42°–44°F, and they are tended by a specialist "cheese master" who turns them, checks their maturity, and makes sure that the store is always stocked.

Marco Gallotta, main chef at both Gusto and Osteria della Frezza, is the man behind the logistics of this gastronomic empire. Although he has to tend daily to the menu for the more than 800-seat capacity of Gusto and the 140-seat La Frezza, he maintains an incredible energy and curiosity towards the art of cooking. Marco says that his main culinary inspiration was his mother, a dilettante cook who always offered her four children a variety of meals, including oysters at a very early age. Although trained professionally as a chef, his credo is for traditional cuisine built on flavor rather than overbearing techniques, with just a few top-notch ingredients. One of his favorite suppliers is understandably Antonio, an 84-year-old man who every Tuesday and Friday comes by train from the nearby village of Zagarolo, carrying precious sacks of *misticanza*, a mix of wild salad leaves and herbs.

Eaten since ancient Roman times and even celebrated in eighteenth-century poems, la misticanza is becoming an endangered salad. Today's younger urban-dwelling generation does not know how to spot edible leaves and relies on the very few remaining old country folk who still wake up at dawn to scour the fields. Misticanza can be an infinite variety of the leaves, the most common being bitter wild chicory, small wild onions, fragrant mint leaves, dandelions, borage, and arugula. Marco uses misticanza as a bed for his delicate pan-fried squid in breadcrumbs and even as a stuffing for his ricotta ravioli.

Another staple of Marco's menu is *cacio e pepe*, the simplest dish ever invented in Roman cuisine – pasta tossed with pecorino romano and freshly ground black pepper. Marco prepares the bowl beforehand by melting the cheese in a little vegetable broth, making sure that all the ingredients are carefully amalgamated. Regardless of minor variations, all of Marco's dishes for Osteria della Frezza tap into the current fascination for simple, gutsy cooking that goes back to the city's roots. The restaurant's *cicchetti*, small portions of whatever is on the menu, recall the Spanish tradition of tapas and have been a further stroke of genius in making this one of Rome's most buzzing places.

angelo fero

Coscio di agnello
Roast leg of lamb

Romans have a predilection for *abbacchio*, the milk-fed lamb known in other parts of Italy as *agnello da latte*. It usually weighs less than 18 lb, so one is often served a dozen tiny chops. The suckling lamb's pink meat is sweeter and milder than a lamb fed on grass, and its delicate taste needs very little adornment. Romans eat abbacchio in a variety of ways: *scottadito*, so called because the grilled chops are piping hot and scald your fingers; *brodettato* with a lemon, egg, and cheese sauce; *alla cacciatora* with anchovies, garlic, and wine vinegar; and *alla romana* with white wine. The easiest recipe is to roast a leg and serve it with plenty of oven-roasted potatoes.

2 oz bacon, finely chopped
4 sprigs thyme, leaves picked
3 garlic cloves, finely chopped
2 3/4 lb leg of lamb
olive oil
2/3 cup dry white wine
1 1/4 lb roasting potatoes, cut into chunks
1 celery stalk, thickly sliced
1 carrot, thickly sliced
a few sprigs of rosemary
a few celery leaves
salt and freshly ground black pepper

Combine the bacon, thyme, and two-thirds of the garlic. Rub the paste over the lamb, then season with salt and pepper. Place the lamb in a roasting pan with some olive oil and wine, and roast in a preheated oven at 400°F for 30 minutes.

Add the potatoes, celery, carrot, the remaining garlic, and the rosemary. Season with salt. Pour the cooking juices from the lamb over the vegetables and cook for another 45 minutes.

When cooked (the meat should be pink), remove from the oven and let the meat rest for 5 minutes. Serve with the potatoes, a generous dose of juices, and a few celery leaves as a garnish.

Fritto alla romana
Roman-style fritters

Italians love their fried dishes, and often an entire meal, from first course to fruit, can be composed of deep-fried ingredients, something which is known as *il grande fritto misto*. Roman cuisine is also full of deep-fried recipes, usually cheaper cuts of meat, bits of cheese, and local vegetables, no doubt influenced by the Jewish *friggitori* of the Ghetto (see Ghetto chapter, page 58). Traditionally, *fritto alla romana* was a hearty mix of artichokes, sheep's brains, and several other morsels of offal, all deep-fried in golden batter. Today's custom is slightly less carnivorous, and usually involves a selection of fried ricotta, zucchini flowers stuffed with mozzarella, cream, and salt cod. I give here a recipe for a lighter type of fried artichokes.

Carciofi fritti
Fried artichokes

2 lemons, halved
4 large artichokes
6 tablespoons olive oil
sea salt

Fill a large bowl with water and add the juice of one lemon. Trim the top 1 in off the artichokes. Snap off the hard outer leaves. Trim the dark fibrous parts and rub the artichokes all over with the remaining lemon halves to prevent blackening. Trim the stem and cut 1 in from the base. Cut the artichokes lengthways into six wedges. Cut out the purple leaves inside and remove the fuzzy choke. Place the wedges in the bowl of water.

Pour enough olive oil into a deep pan to come at least one-third of the way up the side, and bring to a moderate heat. When the oil is hot enough, carefully add the artichoke (in batches) and cook for about 15 minutes. Drain on paper towels. Just before serving, reheat the pan over a moderate heat until the oil is sizzling. Fry the artichokes in batches once again until the leaves are brown and curled. Drain well on paper towels and season with salt to taste.

Cacio e pepe
Pasta with pecorino romano and ground pepper

Cacio e pepe is a dish that needs less rather than more. Traditionally the cacio is pecorino romano, a hard cheese made from milk that comes from sheep pastured on the hills around Rome. It is paler and saltier than the cow's milk cheese parmigiano-reggiano. The Roman saying, *"Ci sta come il cacio sui maccheroni"* – it works just like cacio cheese on top of maccheroni – summarizes the attitude towards the role of this cheese in cooking. For those who find the taste of pecorino too strong, Parmesan cheese works as an excellent substitute, although the best flavor is achieved by using a mixture of both. As with so many pasta recipes without cream, the trick is to toss very "wet" pasta in a warm bowl full of grated cheese. Reserve some of the starchy cooking water from the pasta to *mantecare* (amalgamate) all the ingredients into a perfectly moist consistency.

2 teaspoons black peppercorns
1 lb spaghetti
4 tablespoons coarsely grated pecorino romano or
  Parmesan cheese

Coarsely crush the peppercorns using a mortar and pestle. Cook the spaghetti in boiling salted water until al dente. Warm a large serving bowl with hot water. Reserve a cup of the pasta cooking water, then drain the spaghetti without shaking off the excess water. Pour the warm water from the bowl, then add the spaghetti and toss with the pecorino romano, ground pepper, and some of the cooking water.

Serve on individual plates, adding more grated cheese and freshly ground black pepper to taste.

Spigola al sale
Sea bass in a crust of sea salt

This recipe comes from La Rosetta chef Massimo Riccioli's booklet *A Cena con gli Dei*. It is a classic Mediterranean dish, which can be made with different fish, but works particularly well with sea bass.

1 lb coarse sea salt or Maldon sea salt flakes
2 fresh sea bass, about 1 1/4 lb each, or 1 large one, about 3 lb
extra-virgin olive oil

Cover a baking tray with a layer of coarse sea salt. Wash and dry the fish, and place on the salt. Cover it with another thick layer of salt. Cook in a preheated oven at 400°F for about 25 minutes – less if you have two smaller fish. Check to see whether the fish is cooked by pulling at the spine – if it tears away the fish is cooked.

Take the fish out of the oven and remove the salt crust, the spine, and then the skin. Clean and filet the sea bass, taking care the meat does not come into contact with the salt. Serve drizzled with a little bit of extra-virgin olive oil.

Polpette in umido
Meatballs in tomato sauce

There is an Italian saying that states one should never order *polpette* (meatballs) in restaurants because they are obviously made with yesterday's meat. The Osteria della Frezza's meatballs are a happy exception to the rule – a deliciously simple dish made with fresh ground veal.

2 lb ground veal
1 1/2 tablespoons finely chopped flat-leaf parsley
1 egg, beaten
2 slices day-old white bread, soaked in 3 tablespoons milk
2 tablespoons olive oil
1 carrot, coarsely chopped
1 celery stalk, coarsely chopped
1 small onion, coarsely chopped
1/2 garlic clove, finely chopped
3 1/2 cups ready-made tomato passata
a few sprigs of flat-leaf parsley
salt and freshly ground black pepper

Combine the veal, parsley, egg, and soaked bread in a large bowl. Season with salt and pepper. Mold the mixture into 20 meatballs, and fry gently in a pan with the olive oil, carrot, celery, onion, and garlic. Add the tomato passata and leave to simmer at a low heat for about 20 minutes. Serve with a few sprigs of flat-leaf parsley as a garnish.

Dolci di carnevale – le frappe
Carnival fritters

The Catholic religion always allows for indulgence, provided it comes with hefty sense of guilt and a dose of penitence at the end. Nothing could epitomize Italian Catholic life better than carnival in Rome. The very etymology of the word "carnevale" means that meat is allowed, and this is definitely a period of abundance and gluttony. For 10 days, children deck themselves out in fancy dress for small home parties and parade through the streets throwing multicoloured *coriandoli* (confetti) in the air. Long before the carnival season starts, bakers begin selling delicious dough fritters dusted with confectioners' sugar such as *frappe* and *castagnole*. The frenzy reaches its apotheosis on Mardi Gras, with adults and children gorging themselves on sweets, after which it is all doom and gloom for the 40 days of Lent – *la quaresima* – until the resurrection of Easter.

Serves 6

3 3/8 cups all-purpose flour
1/4 teaspoon salt
2 teaspoons baking powder
2 eggs
2 tablespoons granulated sugar
olive oil
confectioners' sugar for decoration

Sift together the flour, salt , and baking powder. In a separate bowl, beat the eggs and sugar until thick. Gradually beat in the flour mixture and work to a dough. Turn out onto a floured surface. Knead until smooth. (If too soft, add a little more flour.) Cover and let stand for 1 hour.

Divide the dough into two. Roll out paper-thin. Using a serrated-edge pastry wheel, cut into strips 3/4 in wide and 5 in long. Let stand for 10 minutes.

Heat enough olive oil to fill two-thirds of a deep frying pan. When it sizzles, fry the strips in batches until golden and puffed, about 2 minutes. Drain well on paper towels and serve with a dusting of confectioners' sugar.

tra
stev
ere

Trastevere

Trastevere, which lies across the river Tiber from the old center, is another quintessentially Roman area of the city. The residents call themselves the Romani di Roma, the "real Romans," and even though the area is now swamped by tourists and foreigners who have chosen to live there, it still retains an unmistakable and authentic essence. There is a leisurely pace to Trastevere. Turn into any *vicolo* (narrow road) covered with vine trellises or bougainvillea, and sprinkled with rows of laundry hanging from windows, and be transported back to a world centuries old. The Santa Maria church in Trastevere, with its twelfth-century, Byzantine-style, mosaic-lined façade, is the centerpiece of local life. Here in the square, children play with their dogs around the Bramante fountain, while the café crowd sit outside the bars with their morning cappuccino or *spremuta* (freshly squeezed orange juice). It is said that Santa Maria is the oldest church and fountain in Rome, and that on the day Christ was born a fountain of pure oil sprang from the earth. A small road off the piazza is called Via della Fonte Olio in honor of the event. Trastevere was home to the celebrated Roman poets, Giuseppe Gioacchino Belli (1791–1863) and Trilussa (Carlo Alberto Salustri, 1871–1950). Both wrote poems in the *romanesco* dialect; eating and joviality were often their prime subjects. Many restaurants and bars in Trastevere bear the names of these famous sons, as if to certify the traditional authenticity of their fare.

Along with Campo dei Fiori, Trastevere is the *rione* (quarter) that boasts the most restaurants, pizzerias, and bars. In fact, for many Romans, Trastevere is largely a place to go to eat for the evening with your friends. During the summer, the whole city decamps to Trastevere for the *Festa di Noantri*, a festival that was originally held on San Giovanni's Day, 24 June, but that today extends for eight days during July. *Noantri* means "us" – in contrast to *voiatri*, Romans from elsewhere – reinforcing the *trasteverini* notion of being *veraci* (authentic). During Noantri, Trastevere's traffic comes to a standstill, with Romans lining up at stall vendors for roasted nuts, candy, toys, refreshing watermelon slices, and *grattachecca*, Rome's very own granita (see page 51). One of the most popular hang-outs is Ai Marmi, a pizzeria on Viale Trastevere nicknamed *L'Obitorio* (the Morgue) by the patrons because of its marble table tops. In the summer, tables spill out on the pavement, and you will find yourself eating bruschetta elbow to elbow with the other trasteverini. The service here is quick, and communication not aimed at tourists, but prices are still low and the quality exceptionally good.

Back in the narrow Via del Moro is Valzani, a pâtisserie specializing in Roman pastries. The 84-year-old owner, Virginia Valzani, has been running the store since she was 14 and shows no signs of slowing down.

While her son works in the *laboratorio* behind the store, baking pastries and concocting recipes for their mouth-watering chocolates, Virginia scurries back and forth, amusing her faithful customers with a smile and some well-chosen jokes.

Valzani's specialities include *pangiallo*, *mostacciolo romano,* and *panpepato*, sweet treats which carry the ancient Roman tradition of using honey, nuts, and dried fruit rather than sugar. Virginia knows well the history of Roman pâtisserie. Two Roman specialities, *torrone romano* (a variation on the Italian Christmas sweet traditionally made of dried nougat) and *il maritozzo*, made of a breadlike dough and filled with whipped cream, have a phallic shape, she says, because they were originally baked to celebrate ancient Roman weddings. In more recent times, maritozzi acquired the title of *quaresimali*, as they are eaten in the "meager" days before Easter. Pliny the Elder writes about Roman matrons crunching on *mostaccium*, hard sweets made of honey on the steps of the Forum. Having been in the shop since 1924, Virginia has seen trends come and go, and Rome's tastes change, according to economic and cultural influences. For the 1960 Rome Olympics, Valzani created the *torta nanà*, a *semifreddo* made of chocolate and whipped cream the circular shape of which recalls the Olympic logo. When film-maker Nanni Moretti featured the Austrian chocolate *Sachertorte* in his film *Bianca*, customers flocked to the store asking for it. According to Virginia, the custom of baking and eating the Sacher cake really goes back to eighteenth-century Austrian domination of Italy. Today one of her store's most popular chocolates are the *diavoletti*, small pralines made with bitter cocoa and chili, inspired by the recent film *Chocolat* starring a confectionery-making Juliette Binoche.

The history of Roman cooking and that of Trastevere seem intertwined, with many recipes ending with the phrase *alla trasteverina*. Among recipes that carry the area's badge are *melanzane ripiene alla trasteverina* (eggplant stuffed with dried porcini), *pollo alla trasteverina*, *funghi alla trasteverina*, *bruschetta alla trasteverina*, and so on. The nearby Jewish Ghetto, created across the Tiber in 1556, and its cuisine had a strong influence on Trastevere cooking, and it is often difficult to say where the Jewish cuisine ends and the Roman one starts. Another influence was the abundance of fish such as trout and eels, available from the then clean waters of the Tiber as recently as the 1960s. Ada Boni, arguably the most famous Roman cookery writer, mentions rare species such as *la laccia* and *il barbo*, indigenous species of fish that would be boiled, roasted, or slow-cooked with peas.

Similarly to Campo dei Fiori, the food market in Piazza San Cosimato is Trastevere's center for food shopping. Butcher Mauro sells lamb, beef, tripe, and *pajata* (milk-fed veal intestines) for traditional Roman recipes, while vegetable seller Zaira display the freshest zucchini, broccoli, and artichokes. As in most markets, the classification *romanesco* is something to look for. These vegetables come daily from the countryside around Rome and are usually an indigenous variety, remarkably different from the ones found in other parts of Italy. Innocenzi, just off the square, is a spice lover's dream, with sacks of spices, grains, flours, nuts, and pasta stacked against its walls. A row of stores along Via Natale del Grande sells everything the Roman housewife might require, from ricotta cake to slices of fennel-seasoned *porchetta* ham. Further up along Via San

Francesco a Ripa there is the Antica Caciara Trasteverina, so called because it housed the local shepherd's produce. Founded in 1900 and run by Roberto Polica with his sisters, this is a cheese store for locals, the wide selection of which can easily justify its gourmet status. Although they offer specialities from all over Italy, it is their fresh ricotta that steals the show. Brought in from the Lazio countryside at around 6 am, it is usually snapped up by midmorning.

Back on the square, Alberto Ciarla's restaurant is the Trastevere address for Roman high cuisine, specializing in fish and seafood. Ciarla comes from a family of restaurateurs and wine makers from the Castelli area outside of Rome. At one point, at least 50 of his relatives owned several establishments around Rome, often little more than a *fagotteria*, a rustic wine bar where you would bring your own food wrapped into a *fagotto* (parcel) to be served with wine on tap. Ciarla started his culinary career in his parent's restaurant in the 1960s, and soon developed an interest in French cuisine. Roman tradition features strongly in his menu, alongside a few "adapted" variations such as his *fritto antico*, made with baby squid, calamari, and shrimp, or his fish soup (see following recipes). Ciarla is a knowledgeable cook who likes to consult the ancient cooking manuals. Another dish to draw inspiration from the past is *panacea*, a rich seafood and fish platter the recipe of which he adapted from Pope Pius V's chef Bartolomeo Scappi.

A more recent addition to the constellation of Trastevere establishments is the Enoteca Ferrara, a restaurant, wine bar, and food store perched on the corner with Piazza Trilussa. It offers a contemporary take on Italian food with a constantly changing menu of dishes such as swordfish *involtini*, tagliatelle in a duck *ragù* (sauce) and chocolate mousse with wild strawberries. The extensive wine cellar specializes in Italian labels. In the summer, the few outdoor chairs make it a perfect stop for an aperitivo, and there is a selection on the counter of *stuzzichini*, morsels of pizza, fried polenta, and olives, the main function of which is that of *stuzzicare*, that is, to whet your appetite.

Pomodori al riso

Rice-stuffed tomatoes

Although tomatoes were only used in Roman cooking from the seventeenth century onwards, after having been imported from the Americas, it is very difficult to conceive of Roman cooking and indeed most of Italian cooking without this precious ingredient. Stuffed tomatoes with rice is another classic of Roman summer cooking, usually served at room temperature with roasted potatoes or even slightly chilled.

4 large, not-too-ripe firm tomatoes
2 cups risotto rice (Arborio or Vialone Nano will do)
2 tablespoons olive oil
1 garlic clove, chopped
bunch of basil, leaves picked and shredded
bunch of flat-leaf parsley, leaves picked and chopped
5–6 desalted capers (the tinier the better)
1 1/4 lb roasting potatoes, cut into chunks
salt and freshly ground black pepper

Slice off the tops of the tomatoes and set aside. Remove all the seeds and some of the dividing walls, leaving just three or four large sections. Salt lightly and put the tomatoes open end down in a dish, allowing any excess liquid to drain away.

Parboil the rice in a pot of boiling salted water until al dente. Drain and mix in a bowl with the olive oil, garlic, basil, parsley, and capers. Let the mixture marinate for about 20 minutes.

Place the tomatoes on an oiled baking sheet, fill them to the brim with the rice mixture and replace the tops. Place the potatoes around the tomatoes, and bake in a preheated oven at 400°F for about 1 hour.

La Grattachecca

Fruit-flavored ice crush

During the warm Roman summer evenings, stall sellers along the river Tiber sell ripe watermelons and *grattachecca*, a syrupy type of granita, to quench the thirst of passers-by. With a special spoon, the seller scrapes from a block of ice until he has filled a glass with crushed ice. He then adds a dash of fruit syrup – anything from cherry to lemon or barley flavor.

8 oz crushed ice
3 tablespoons barley water, or orange or lemon syrup

Take some ice cubes from the freezer, leave them on the worktop for a short while to melt slightly and then briefly crush them in a blender. Add the syrup to the crushed ice and serve immediately.

Pasta alla checca

Pasta checca-style

Pasta alla checca is a typical Roman pasta dish that is easy to make and usually cooked in the summer when it is far too hot to be hanging around the kitchen stove. It makes a great picnic dish and is often made for a day out at the beach.

8–10 vine-ripened cherry tomatoes
1 tablespoon desalted capers
1 garlic clove
about 15 basil leaves
3 1/2 oz pitted black olives
good-quality olive oil
1 lb short pasta, either conchiglie (shells), half rigatoni, bombolotti, or fusilli
1 1/8 cups (4 oz) cow's milk mozzarella, shredded

Bring a large pot of salted water to a boil. Quickly blanch the tomatoes, then dice them. In a large serving bowl, mix the tomato with the capers (which must be soaked if they have been salted), garlic clove, half of the basil leaves, and the olives. Drizzle plenty of olive oil and mix all the ingredients together. Leave them to marinate for a good 40 minutes.

Cook the pasta until al dente, and toss in the bowl with the tomato mixture. Wait until the pasta has cooled, then add the mozzarella. Keep the pasta in the refrigerator and take out 20 minutes before serving to adjust to room temperature. Garnish with the remaining basil leaves and serve.

Zuppa di pasta e fagioli ai frutti di mare

Pasta and borlotti bean soup with seafood

This is another of Alberto Ciarla's specialities that combines the typical Roman pasta and bean soup with seafood. I have omitted from the recipe all the seafood not readily available outside Italy, although it does need to be fresh.

5 oz borlotti beans, soaked for 12 hours, then rinsed, or 13 oz canned beans, drained and rinsed
1 carrot, chopped
1 celery stalk, chopped
5 tablespoons olive oil
7 oz clams
7 oz mussels
2/3 cup dry white wine
2 oz bacon, chopped
1/2 onion, thinly sliced
2 garlic cloves, peeled and left whole
5 oz canned tomatoes
5 oz shelled shrimp
5 oz cleaned baby squid
7 oz small pasta shapes such as maccheroni
salt and freshly ground black pepper

Boil the soaked borlotti beans until they are tender, then drain. Fry gently in a pan with the celery and carrot for 5 minutes with 1 tablespoon of the oil.

Put the clams and mussels in another pan over a low heat, add 2 tablespoons of water and the wine. Cover with a lid until the shells are wide open. Remove the clams and mussels from the shells, discarding any that stay closed.

Gently fry the bacon, garlic, and onion in a pan with 3 tablespoons of the olive oil. Discard the garlic. Add the tomatoes, clams, mussels, shrimp, and squid. Season, then increase the heat to moderate and simmer until cooked.

Meanwhile cook the pasta in a pan of salted boiling water until al dente. Drain and toss with the seafood over low heat. Add the bean mixture, drizzle with the remaining olive oil and serve immediately.

Crostini con alici e mozzarella

Crostini with anchovies and mozzarella

Crostini alla provatura are toasted slices of crusty bread that Romans like to cover with butter, melted cheese, and anchovies. Favorite cheeses are *caciocavallo*, provolone, and smoked *provola*, all being Lazio cheeses that work well as toppings because they melt into delicious creamy fondues. Crostini are traditionally served as starters.

4 large slices crusty bread
4 or 5 anchovy filets, preserved in oil
7 tablespoons butter
10 oz good melting cheese such as provola or caciocavallo,
** sliced**

Toast the bread slices in a pre-heated oven at 350°F or under the broiler. Drain the anchovies from the oil on some paper towels. Chop thinly and add to a heated pan with the butter, crushing them with a wooden spoon so they break up. Pour the butter and anchovies over the bread slices, and top each one with a slice of cheese. Place them on a baking sheet and broil until the cheese has melted.

Fritto antico

Ancient Rome-style fried seafood platter

Alberto Ciarla says he invented this spurious recipe by trying to figure out how poor Romans of the past would cook a seafood dish. His answer was to use semolina, rather than the more precious ingredient of eggs, to coat the seafood. He seasons the fresh baby squid, calamari, and shrimp with a selection of herbs, then fries them in olive oil.

7 oz fresh baby squid, cleaned
7 oz fresh calamari rings
13 oz fresh shelled shrimp
2 1/4 cups semolina flour
3 tablespoons dried herbs such as marjoram or oregano
olive oil for frying
1 lemon, cut into wedges, for serving
salt

Put the cleaned seafood onto paper towels or a clean tea towel to absorb any remaining water. Coat all the seafood in semolina flour, then season with salt and the dried herbs.

Pour enough olive oil into a deep frying pan or skillet to fill it a third of the way up the sides, then place over a high heat. When the oil is sizzling hot, quickly dip the seafood in a bowl of water before placing carefully in the pan. Fry the seafood in batches – about 3 minutes for each batch – taking care to place it on kitchen paper to absorb all the oil after frying. Serve hot with a few lemon wedges.

ghetto e isola

tib

erina

Ghetto & Isola Tiberina

The Jewish Ghetto is the area in Rome that most feels like a village. On weekends, especially in the spring and summer, as the sun sets and the traffic roar dies down, clusters of locals meet for an early evening chat, perched on the steps or seated at the outdoor tables of one of the cafés. Children roam freely in the pedestrian area, and everybody seems to know each other by first name. The kosher restaurants fill up with their first sittings, usually Northern European tourists with early eating habits, crunching crispy golden fried artichokes under the setting of the Portico of Octavia.

The history of the Roman Jews is a long and sad one. The oldest Jewish community in the Western world, they came to Rome in 161 BC when representatives sought protection from the Syrians. Many Jews decided to stay in Rome because it was a good trade center. As the emperors started to take over Palestine, so too, did their persecution of the Jewish people increase. The Jews rebelled and Rome responded violently, destroying the second temple of Jerusalem in AD 70 and effectively spearheading the Jewish diaspora for the next 1900 years. Unlike the Sephardic Jews, who went to Moorish Spain, and the Ashkenazi, who travelled to Northern or Eastern Europe, Roman Jews speak neither Landino nor Yiddish, but rather have their own culture and language, a mix of Hebrew and Italian.

In the Middle Ages, their industry and financial capacity meant that the popes tolerated their presence and even allowed them to build a synagogue in the city. As the Vatican increased its power, however, anti-Jewish propaganda grew, and in the thirteenth century, Pope Innocent III made the Jews wear distinguishing mark, a yellow "O." In 1555, Pope Paul IV issued a decree that forced all Jews to live in a ghetto next to the river Tiber, and even imposed a curfew. The area, then a tangle of insalubrious narrow, dark roads and secret squares, is contained between the Via Arenula, the Theater of Marcellus, and the riverbank of the Tiber. It was in this period that most of Jewish cooking defined itself – a simple cuisine born out of a "siege mentality" and a lack of choice. Cheap cuts of meat would be stewed for hours until tender, simple salads such as curly endive (frisée) cooked and seasoned with olives and anchovies, easy-to-preserve salt cod battered and deep-fried, cakes spiced with plenty of cinnamon and nutmeg. Street vendors would fry all sorts of *pezzetti fritti* – scraps of broccoli, apples, and zucchini – and sell *le coppiette* – dried horsemeat strips. Many dishes inevitably end with

Opposite: The Tiberina island rises between the Trastevere and the old Jewish Ghetto area. On it is the large Fatebene Fratelli hospital and one of Rome's most celebrated establishments, the restaurant Sora Lella.

Food lovers' address book

Sora Lella (restaurant)
Via Ponte Quattro Capi 16
tel +39 06 6861601

Antico Forno del Ghetto (bakery)
Piazza Costaguti 30–31
tel +39 06 68803012

Zi Fenizia (pizzeria)
Via S. Maria del Pianto 64–65
tel +39 06 6896976

Ristorante Kosher (restaurant)
Via Portico d'Ottavio 8
tel +39 06 68809771

Giggetto a Portico d'Ottavia
(restaurant)
Via del Portico d'Ottavia 21/a
tel +39 06 6861105

Marco Latella (butchery)
Via S. Maria del Pianto 61
tel +39 06 6864659

Antico Forno Cordella (bakery)
Piazza Costaguti 30/31
tel +39 06 68803012

Il Pompiere (restaurant)
Via S. Maria dei Calderari 38
tel +39 06 6868377

Dolce Roma (pâtisserie)
Via Portico d'Ottavia 20b
tel +39 06 6892196

Sora Margherita (restaurant)
Piazza delle Cinque Scole 30
tel +39 06 6864002

the phrase *alla giudia* – Jewish-style. Among these, Giuliano Malizia, author of a book on Jewish Roman cuisine, lists *polpette alla giudia* (meatballs with egg and nutmeg), *melanzane alla giudia* (eggplant fried with garlic) and, of course, *carciofi alla giudia* (deep-fried flattened artichokes).

Up to 1870 the Jews were forbidden from owning land or practicing any kind of trade other than the selling of rags and scrap iron. They finally enjoyed a short period of freedom under Napoleon and the Roman Republic, when the Jewish community flourished and built the Temple of Rome, a majestic marble structure with one of the most prominent domes in the city. The Jews suffered persecution again under the hands of Mussolini's Fascist regime in the 1930s. which issued laws that excluded them from schools and professions. In 1943, the SS who invaded Rome told the rabbi that the community would be ransomed if it did not collect 50 kg (110 lb) of gold. On 16 October, two weeks after the collection, the SS raided the Ghetto, rounded up 2091 Jews and deported them. Only 15 returned. Until a few years ago, some of the survivors could still be encountered, as they went about their daily business in the Ghetto, their concentration-camp numbers indelibly tattooed on their arms.

Today, there are 16,000 Jews in Rome, either descendants from previous generations or originating from Tripoli in Libya. The most lively area in the Ghetto is along the Via Portico d'Ottavia, a jam-packed strip full of kosher food shops, pizzerias, bakeries, and bars. On the corner is the Pasticceria Boccioni, a bakery that has been churning out Jewish pastries from its cramped premises for 90 years. Always slightly burnt but nevertheless delicious are the chewy honey almond biscuits, sweet Jewish pizza with crystallized fruits and pine nuts eaten at weddings and births, fragrant ricotta and chocolate cakes, and warm toasted buttersquash seeds, the so-called *bruscolini*. Next door, the bakery called Antico Forno del Ghetto bakes *pizza bianca* and *pizza rossa* every 15 minutes. Zi Fenizia is a *pizzeria al taglio* serving sliced pizza with more than 30 types of kosher topping without cheese, such as marinated zucchini or endive and anchovies. Further up the street is the kosher butcher Giacomo, and Marco Latella, another top-rate butcher selling steak for *fiorentina*, roast beef, veal, and kidneys.

In the Piazza delle Cinque Scole is Sora Margherita, a tiny restaurant with no outdoor sign. Since 1927 it has served a plate and a glass of Velletri wine to the *popolino*, the working-class inhabitants of the city. Today its paper-cloth tables are graced by locals, students, and even the odd MP on a lunch break. Sora Margherita has recently changed management after the "Sora" (which in *romanesco* dialect means "Mrs") Margherita retired; however, very little has changed. Every morning at 6 am, 100 fresh eggs are delivered and the Signora Gianna arrives to make fresh fettuccine, *agnolotti*, gnocchi, and *maltagliati* pasta. Cook Lucia, who used to work with Margherita, now runs the kitchen, serving classics such as pasta and *ceci* (chickpea and pasta soup), *baccalà in guazzetto* (salt cod in a sauce made with tomatoes, pine nuts, and raisins) and Roman-style tripe. She even cooks "variations on the theme," such as macaroni with ricotta instead of cacio cheese and ground black pepper, or polenta with kosher veal sausages.

Just across the square, housed in a frescoed palazzo once the home of courtesan Beatrice Cenci, is Il Pompiere, a family-run establishment serving all the dishes of a traditional Roman restaurant plus different soups every day of the week. Monday is the turn of pasta and broccoli, Tuesday it is pasta and beans, Wednesday is spelt soup, Thursday is gnocchi, and Friday is pasta and chickpeas.

Back on the Via Portico d'Ottavio is the Ristorante Kosher, serving a great fresh tagliatelle pasta with artichokes and grouper, and chicory with *bottarga* (smoked cod roe), a delicacy that has always been a staple of Jewish cuisine, but has only recently been elevated by other cuisines to the status of a refined ingredient. Just underneath the portico is the Gigetto restaurant, a Roman institution since the 1920s and famed – regardless of its Catholic owners – for the carciofi alla giudia. Next door to Gigetto, his parent's restaurant, Stefano Ceccarelli opened Dolce Roma a few years ago, a pâtisserie that combines traditional Jewish sweets such as ricotta and cherry cheesecake with rich American- and Austrian-style pastries such as *Sachertorte*, strudel, and muffins.

Walking along past the synagogue and across the footbridge you come to Isola Tiberina, a small, tranquil island perched on the river Tiber. Today it is the home to the large hospital of Fatebene Fratelli, the church of Saint Bartolomeo, a bar serving mostly hospital staff, and Sora Lella's restaurant, perhaps one of the most celebrated Roman establishments. A formidable, rather large, humorous woman, Sora Lella was the sister of Roman actor Aldo Fabrizi, who starred in many Neo-Realist films. Sora Lella opened the restaurant in the 1959, and it soon became a hang-out of film stars and occasional tourists. She has also written a book of Roman recipes with her brother Aldo, also a good cook, which reads more like a collection of romanesco poems.

Although Sora Lella and her brother Aldo have unfortunately passed away, their spirit and cooking are still kept well alive by Sora Lella's son Aldo Trabalza and his three sons. Aldo mixes his own curries, blends Maldon sea salt flakes with wild herbs, makes marmalades and chutneys to serve with cheeses, employs a wide choice of dried fruits and nuts in his recipes, and cooks one of the best versions of Icelandic salt cod on the market. All this while never forgetting to find first-rate local ingredients such as sheep's milk ricotta and milk-fed lamb from the neighboring Lazio countryside, creating a cuisine that is both traditional and refined.

Carciofo alla giudia
Jewish-style artichokes

Nothing is more satisfying than biting into a warm, crunchy *carciofo alla giudia*, whole artichokes flattened and deep-fried until golden. Although eaten in large quantities in almost every Roman restaurant, this dish is rarely served at home, perhaps because it can be quite tricky to get absolutely right without professional equipment. The secret is to fry the artichokes twice and spray them in between with ice-cold water. The second frying will make the artichokes open up their petals like a flower. It is best to fry one artichoke at a time.

4 tender globe artichokes
1 lemon, halved
plenty of extra-virgin olive oil
salt to taste

Fill a large bowl with enough water to cover the artichokes, and squeeze the juice of 1/2 lemon into it. Cut off the top 1 in of the artichokes, leaving the stems attached. Snap off all the hard outer leaves until you reach the tender, pale yellow ones. Trim away the dark, fibrous parts and remove the choke. Rub them all over with the remaining lemon half to prevent blackening. Trim the artichoke stem and cut off 1 in at the base. If not frying immediately, keep the artichokes in the bowl of acidulated water.

Pour at least 5 in of olive oil into a tall, narrow saucepan. Place over a medium heat until the oil is piping hot but not smoking. One at time, immerse each artichoke in the hot oil for 8–10 minutes, so that it floats, turning it over so all parts are cooked. Drizzle with some water to increase crispiness. Remove from the pan and drain well on paper towels. Let the artichokes cool for 10 minutes.

Add some fresh oil to the pan and bring to piping-hot heat again. Lower each artichoke into the pan – again one at a time – and fry until all the leaves have opened and turned golden. Remove from the pan, drain again on absorbent kitchen paper. Sprinkle with salt and serve hot.

Aliciotti con indivia
Anchovies with curly endive

Anchovies have been a staple of the city since ancient times. In Rome, they go by the name of *alici* or *aliciotti*, *acciughe* when salted and *pasta d'acciuga* when made into paste. David Downie writes in his Roman Anchovy article that many Roman writers chronicled the popularity of this fish. They described how patricians and slaves devoured anchovies both fresh and salted and fermented in sauces, brines, and pastes such as the foul-smelling *garum*. Still today, Romans use anchovies as condiments, for salad dressings (see recipe for puntarelle salad on page 18), as stuffing for zucchini flowers, or as toppings for pizza. This is a classic Jewish Roman recipe adapted by the Sora Margherita restaurant in the Ghetto. *L'indivia* is a typical bitter chicory found in the Lazio countryside, similar to French curly endive (frisée) and used extensively both raw and cooked. A good trick is to blanch the salad leaves beforehand to rid them of their bitter taste.

3 lbindivia or curly endive (frisée)
olive oil
1 3/4 lb large fresh anchovies, cleaned and fileted, heads removed
2 garlic cloves, finely chopped
1 fresh or dried red chili, deseeded and finely chopped
1/2 cup dry white wine
2 tablespoons dried breadcrumbs
salt and freshly ground black pepper

Blanch the endive in a pot of salted boiling water, then drain well. Cover the bottom of a baking dish with a film of olive oil. Place half the anchovies in a layer in the dish, then sprinkle over the garlic and chili, and season with salt and pepper. Place a layer of endive on top. Repeat with another layer both of fish and salad. Pour the wine over the layers, and sprinkle with the breadcrumbs.

Place in a preheated oven at 400°F, and allow to cook for at least 30 minutes. Quickly grill the top under a hot broiler until the breadcrumbs turn golden. Serve warm.

Brasato di maialino in agrodolce antica roma

Roast pork loin in a sweet and sour sauce

This is obviously not a Jewish recipe, but one which belongs to Sora Lella, the restaurant located on the Isola Tiberina, facing the synagogue. It is my favorite Sora Lella dish. The use of dried prunes and apricots is a nod to the ancient Rome tradition, as well as a reflection of Sora Lella owner Aldo Trabalza's passion for dried fruit and nuts. The sweet and sour sauce is typical of Roman cuisine.

1 lb fresh pork loin
1 slice pancetta or smoked bacon
3 celery stalks
3 carrots
4 dried prunes, pitted
4 dried apricots
1 tablespoon raisins
1 tablespoon pine nuts
1 teaspoon shelled whole pistachio nuts
1 teaspoon slivered almonds
3 small onions
olive oil
about 1 1/2 cup dry white wine

For the seasoning
1 teaspoon fennel seed
1 teaspoon dried marjoram or a few fresh leaves
a few sage leaves
a few rosemary sprigs
2 bay leaves, fresh or dried
1 teaspoon dried oregano or a few fresh leaves
sprinkle of ground nutmeg
2 cloves
a few juniper berries, crushed
3 garlic cloves, thinly sliced
salt and freshly ground black pepper

For the sauce
2 tablespoons granulated sugar
1/2 glass white wine vinegar
2 tablespoons flour
salt

Lay the pork loin flat on a work surface, and season the surface of the meat with all the seasoning ingredients. Put the pancetta slice on top, then slice one of the celery stalks and one of the carrots and place on top of the pancetta. Next add the prunes, apricots, raisins, pine nuts, pistachio nuts, and almonds. Roll the pork loin on itself and tie in position with string.

Place the pork in an ovenproof dish. Chop the remaining celery and carrots, and the onions, and add to the dish. Pour some olive oil and enough white wine to cover the meat a third of the way up its sides.

Brown the meat on one side in a preheated oven at 500°F for about 30 minutes or less, then turn over and brown on the other side for another 30 minutes. Stick a fork in the meat; if there is a lot of juice coming out, roast for another hour at 350°F. If you like the meat quite pink and there is not too much juice coming out of it, you can cook it for just another 20 minutes. Take the meat out of the oven and leave to rest a few minutes.

Remove the meat from its baking dish and place in the refrigerator, making sure that you collect all the cooking juices in a separate container. Add some water to the juices, stir through and put in the refrigerator as well. Take the container out 30 minutes before you wish to serve the pork and skim off the film of fat on top.

Pour the juices into a clean saucepan over a medium-low heat; before it warms, add the sugar, vinegar, and salt to create a sweet-and-sour flavor. Sprinkle in the flour and stir to create a sauce with the consistency of yogurt. Remove the pan from the heat and push the sauce through a sieve. Set aside.

In the meantime, remove the pork loin from the refrigerator. Either reheat it sliced in a baking dish, or in a pan with a bit of water and the sauce. Serve with extra cooked prunes and a few sweet and sour onions (see recipe in San Lorenzo chapter, page 74).

Crostata di ricotta e visciole

Ricotta cheesecake with cherries

This is the quintessential Jewish cheesecake that is found in restaurants and pâtisseries everywhere in Rome. It combines buttery, sweet sheep's milk ricotta cheese with the tart taste of wild cherries. *Pasta frolla*, a sweet egg pastry, covers the cake completely. A variation is also with chocolate flakes.

Serves 10

For the pastry
2 1/4 cups all-purpose flour
1/2 cup granulated sugar
1 3/8 stick (10 1/2 tablespoons) unsalted butter at room temperature, cut into small chunks
2 egg yolks, beaten
grated zest of 1 lemon
pinch of salt

For the filling
13 oz fresh sheep's milk or other ricotta
1/4 cup granulated sugar
1 egg, beaten
3 tablespoons cherry jam or conserve (or chocolate broken into small chunks)
confectioners' sugar to decorate

To make the pastry, pour the flour onto a cool work surface and make a well in the center. Put the remaining pastry ingredients into the well and mix together, kneading them briefly. As soon as they are amalgamated into a compact dough, wrap the dough in waxed paper or plastic wrap. Place in the refrigerator and leave for about 1 hour before proceeding with the rest of the recipe – the dough can be refrigerated for up to 5 hours.

If you wish, you can prepare the dough in a food processor or a mixer with a dough hook. Place all the ingredients in the bowl, and process off and on until balls of dough form on the blades or hook. Remove the dough from the food processor and shape it into a single ball before wrapping and refrigerating it.

Divide the dough into two unequal pieces, one-third and two-thirds. Roll out the larger piece of dough to a circle about 1/4 in thick and 11 inches in diameter. Use to line a greased and floured pie dish, 10 inches in diamter, trimming any excess dough with a knife. Prick the dough with a fork and set aside.

Prepare the filling by combining the ricotta, sugar, and egg until well blended. Using a spatula, spread the cherry jam over the pastry base (if you are using chocolate instead of jam, simply sprinkle it over the base). Cover it with a thick layer of the ricotta mixture.

Roll out the remaining third of pastry and cut into strips 1 in thick with a serrated pastry wheel. Lay the strips over the ricotta to resemble a grid of crossed lines.

Bake the cheesecake in a preheated oven at 425°F for 1 hour until the top pastry strips are golden. Remove from the oven and allow to cool, then place in the refrigerator for at least 2 hours. Serve in slices with a dusting of confectioners' sugar on top.

san
lorenzo

San Lorenzo

San Lorenzo was one of the very few areas of Rome to be bombed during World War II. The Pope's presence had meant that the city had regarded itself as immune from devastation. Instead, on 19 July 1943, American planes dropped bombs and killed 3000 people, paradoxically in the part of the city in which the most vehement opponents to the Mussolini regime lived. Today, memories of the bombing can still be found in the large damaged houses that have been left empty and never rebuilt.

Dubbed by the Romans themselves as the city's equivalent to Soho, San Lorenzo has over the past years built itself a reputation as the "happening" area, where students, artists, and designers live, work, and play. The core of San Lorenzo remains authentically working class, with Roma football supporters' clubs, anarchist book stores, a buzzing food market, and old restaurants still serving traditional dishes. But a recent spate of wine bars and clubs, as well as the presence nearby of *centri sociali* (occupied squats) which have been turned into thriving cultural centers running concerts and festivals, gives the area a youthful and creative feel.

One of the first "contemporary food" restaurants to open in San Lorenzo in the late 1980s, the Tram Tram restaurant, owes its name to the interior décor which employs disused train parts, as well as the restaurant's proximity to the train line. But above all the railway reference is a historical one, as at the beginning of the nineteenth century San Lorenzo was where railway workers lived. The menu here has a Southern Italian influence for the first courses, while the main dishes are decidedly inspired by Roman cuisine. The small *orecchiette* pasta (named after their shape, which is similar to small ears) is teamed with broccoli and clams, while anchovies and endive salad are served as a terrine.

When Uno e Bino opened in 1997, the brother and sister team behind it, Gianpaolo and Gloria Gravina, were inspired by the atmosphere of Parisian bistros. Uno e Bino's opening was timely, as it followed the rise of the *enoteca* formula, a mix between a restaurant and a wine bar, with a focus on Italian wine labels and creative, rustic cuisine. The enoteca movement reconfigured Rome's gastronomic map in the early 1980s and was largely represented by a team of wine enthusiasts who opened Cul de Sac in the Piazza Navona area, La Bottega del Vino in the Ghetto area, and Il Goccetto in Via dei Banchi Vecchi. The movement was largely spurred by the support of Gambero Rosso, the Rome-based gastronomic publisher and broadcaster that

Opposite: Mobile fruit and vegetable stalls vendors like these are a common sight in the streets of Rome. This one visits San Lorenzo regularly, bellowing through a megaphone to advertize its cheap and fresh produce to the local housewives.

today publishes one of the most influential food guides about Italy. Although Uno e Bino's name derives from a play on a semiotic study of the Pinocchio character, the food served here is not pretentious. The focus is on using top-notch ingredients and referring to Roman tradition, such as tagliatelle with oxtail meat sauce and *baccalà mantecato con crema di ceci* (salt cod with a chickpea cream sauce). Eggs come from organic farms, pistachio nuts come directly from Bronte in Sicily, and the salt cod from Venice. Gianpaolo, who has since left the restaurant management to his sister Gloria in order to concentrate on his philosophy doctorate, has nonetheless kept his passion for wines intact and is now writing wine guides for the Italian publication L'Espresso.

Not far from Uno e Bino is the Paci *pasticceria* in Via Marsi, a local store producing excellent cakes and pastries. Specialities include the traditional *crostata*, with ricotta, lemon, or jam filling, as well as *biscotterie da tè*, small cookies produced for afternoon tea.

But the crown for San Lorenzo's most famous restaurant goes to Pommidoro, which already in the 1970s was a favorite among intellectuals such as the Italian film-maker Pierpaolo Pasolini. Today, Pommidoro is experiencing a second "youth" and is patronized by members of the artist community who live in the nearby *pastificio Cerere* (an old pasta factory and mill converted into studio spaces), as well as by Roma's football team. The restaurant's strength lies in its dishes from the Roman tradition. *Spaghetti alla gricia* (with cured pork jowl), *spaghetti alla carbonara,* and the grilled meat selection are all tasty and well executed. For devoted customers it is also sometimes possible to order *rigatoni alla pajata*, made with milk-fed veal intestines and effectively outlawed by EU regulations since the BSE scare. My advice is to close your eyes to this and taste the delicacy – you won't regret it.

Spaghetti ajo e olio

Spaghetti with garlic and olive oil

A simple dish born out of very few ingredients, this garlicky pasta dish needs top-notch olive oil, preferably dark green fruity oil from the Sabine hills around Rome, to become truly delicious. Some Romans call for this dish to be served without Parmesan cheese, but I find it adds another welcome flavor.

4 garlic cloves, sliced
2 fresh or dried red chilies, deseeded and shredded
3 tablespoons extra-virgin olive oil
1 lb spaghetti
freshly chopped flat-leaf parsley leaves (optional)
freshly grated Parmesan cheese (optional)

Bring a large pot of salted water to a boil. In a large frying pan or skillet, fry the garlic and chilies in the oil over a medium heat for about 1 minute. When the garlic is colored, remove the pan from heat and set aside. Remove the garlic and chilies.

Cook the spaghetti until al dente. Drain and toss the spaghetti in oil in the frying pan over a medium heat for 1 minute. Serve in bowls immediately, sprinkled with parsley and Parmesan, if using.

Spaghetti alla gricia

Spaghetti with bacon

Pommidoro's fame is based on many classic Roman dishes, but the restaurant's *tonnarelli alla gricia* is arguably one of the best in town. The dish's main ingredient is *gricia*, the Roman word for *guanciale*, which might be sold as "cured pork jowl" or "hog mawls." It is a popular ingredient in Roman cuisine and often used to prepare carbonara sauce. Both bacon and pancetta are good substitutes if you cannot find it. If you prefer a smoky taste, try the recipe with streaky bacon or *pancetta affumicata* instead. I have substituted the tonnarelli with spaghetti, which are easier to find.

8 slices guanciale or pancetta
1/2 fresh red chili, deseeded and finely chopped, or
1/4 teaspoon red pepper flakes
1 lb tonnarelli or spaghetti
freshly grated pecorino romano or Parmesan cheese
freshly ground black pepper

Bring a large pot of salted water to a boil. Fry the guanciale and the chili in a large frying pan or skillet until the guanciale is crisp. Remove the pan from the heat.

Meanwhile, cook the spaghetti until al dente. Return the frying pan to medium heat, and drain the spaghetti, reserving some of the cooking water. Toss the pasta in the pan, adding a little bit of the cooking water to keep moist. Season with pepper, then serve in bowls immediately, with plenty of pecorino.

Cipolline in agrodolce
Sweet and sour onions

A classic Roman *contorno* (side dish) that works well with meat. The sweet and sour flavor is reminiscent of ancient Roman cooking.

10 oz shallots or small onions, peeled and left whole
a little olive oil
2 bay leaves
1 tablespoon granulated sugar
scant 1/2 cup white wine vinegar

Brown the shallots in a pan with a little olive oil and the bay leaves. Stir in the sugar and white wine vinegar. Cook gently over medium-low heat, continuing to stir, until the onions have caramelized – about 10-15 minutes. Remove the bay leaves before serving. Serve hot or cold.

Paccheri con ragu di maiale e ricotta
Pasta with pork and ricotta sauce

This recipe comes from Uno e Bino's chef Andrea Buscema, who has carved himself a reputation for serving innovative cuisine with hearty, simple flavors. Andrea's trick is to use buffalo milk ricotta, which is not readily available outside of Italy. Yet by marinating cow's milk ricotta slightly in marjoram leaves one can aspire to reaching a similar delicate flavor. The recipe calls for *paccheri*, a type of pasta from the south of Italy, but it works equally well with rigatoni.

1 tablespoon chopped marjoram leaves, plus extra whole
  leaves to garnish
5 oz ricotta
1 onion, chopped
1 celery stalk, chopped
1 carrot, chopped
olive oil
8 oz ground pork
2/3 cup red wine
13 oz canned tomatoes, or 6–7 large peeled vine-ripened
  tomatoes, chopped
1/2 teaspoon ground cinnamon
1 lb paccheri or rigatoni
salt

Mix the marjoram with the ricotta and allow to marinate for about 15 minutes.

Gently fry the onion, celery, and carrot in a little olive oil in a pan. Add the pork and brown, turning it well with a wooden spoon. Pour in the red wine and when it has evaporated add the tomatoes. Season with salt and the cinnamon. Cook the sauce at a low heat for 30 minutes.

Cook the pasta until al dente in a large pot of salted boiling water. Drain and toss the pasta with the meat sauce. Serve immediately in bowls, with the ricotta sprinkled over the top and extra marjoram leaves as a garnish.

Guancette di manzo
Braised beef cheeks

Another recipe from Uno e Bino's chef Andrea Buscema – this one is a nod to the tradition of the *quinto quarto* cooking of Testaccio (see pages 88–99), where cheap meat cuts are braised until meltingly tender. Andrea serves the beef cheeks on a buttery mash of potatoes, but they also go very well with sweet and sour onions (see recipe page 74).

4 beef cheeks, trimmed of excess fat, about 1 1/2 lb
2 tablespoons olive oil
a few rosemary sprigs, chopped
a few sage leaves, chopped
a few marjoram leaves, chopped
1 carrot, chopped
1 onion, chopped
1/2 celery stalk, chopped
1/2 teaspoon unsweetened cocoa powder
1 1/2 cups red wine
13 oz canned peeled plum tomatoes
4 1/4 cups water
salt and freshly ground black pepper

Brown the beef in a wide heavy pot with no oil, then add the olive oil, herbs, carrot, onion, celery, and cocoa, scraping away any brown bits. Pour in the red wine and allow it to evaporate. Add the tomatoes with juice. Cook over a moderately low heat for 10–15 minutes. Add 4 1/4 cups water, stir through and cover the pan with a lid. Bring to a simmer, then braise gently for about 2 1/2 hours until the sauce is concentrated and the meat very tender. Season with salt and pepper just before serving.

Pesche al vino bianco
Peaches in white wine

This fruit dessert is made everywhere in Italy, but finds in Rome an ideal interpretation thanks to a large, local variety of yellow peach called Flaminia. Simple and delicious, it is the perfect end to a meal.

4 large yellow peaches, sliced
1 1/2 cups dry white wine
2 teaspoons granulated sugar

Simply dunk the peach slices in the wine and sprinkle with the sugar – that's it.

monti e esquilino

Monti e Esquilino

As Rome property prices soar and apartments in the center are harder to come by, Monti and Esquilino have undergone a recent revival as desirable postcodes. Monti, the area between the Coliseum and Via Nazionale, is one of Rome's oldest *rioni* (quarters). During the Roman Empire it was called *La Suburra* (inhabited area under the city) and famed for being a poor, overcrowded, and dangerous place. This was where Nero would come incognito to test the populace's moods, while Claudius's promiscuous wife Messalina would search for pleasure in one of the many brothels. Today, antique shops, wine bars, and trattorie line the medieval streets, helping to maintain its lively reputation. Just beyond the Basilica of Santa Maria Maggiore, one of Rome's four patriarchal basilicas, starts the Esquilino, Rome's highest hill. For years, this area was dominated by the neighboring presence of the central railway station and the constant flow of African and Chinese immigrants. The wholesale market, previously found in the center square, Piazza Vittorio, and now relocated to nearby Via Filippo Turati, is the hub of a lively international food trade, with stalls selling anything from *romanesco* vegetables to spices, yams, and halal-butchered meat. Today the Roman middle class who have snapped up the 1870s-built palazzi cohabit with a populous Chinese community. Foodwise, the Esquilino combines classic Roman institutions with more "exotic" offerings, from mainly Oriental and Ethiopian restaurants.

Esquilino's most popular store is Panella, the tag line of which, "The art of the bread," summarizes its dedication to this essential food. Bakers since 1920, the Panella family has researched the subject in detail, and sells around 80 varieties of bread. Bread with herbs (rosemary, arugula, and sage); crunchy, wafer-thin Sardinian bread; Jewish *azzimo* bread without yeast; crusty Roman *pane casareccio*; and baguettes are just some of the items from which to choose. During Carnevale, Panella sells chocolate *frappe*, while for Easter there are the traditional dove-shaped *colombe* cakes, *pastiere napoletane,* and cheese pizzas. Even pastries of the sort found in the Pompeii archeological sites are on sale, as well as recipes mentioned by Pliny the Elder.

Close by is the Pasticceria Regoli, famed for its *millefoglie* star-shaped cake, *la stella*. Regoli was started in 1919 by Umberto and Narcisa Ficini, a couple who had moved to Rome from Pisa in search of fortune. At the time, Esquilino was a populous area, and the wholesale market was a place where stockists attracted buyers and businessmen from all over the region. Out of necessity, Narcisa trained as a pastry chef, and her store became so successful that it allegedly spurred many other Tuscan friends and relatives to transfer

Opposite: The Basilica of Santa Maggiore effectively stands as a divide between the Monti and the Esquilino area.

themselves to Rome and open pastry stores. Today, third-generation Carlo Regoli and his wife, Laura, run Regoli. Aside from the millefoglie, the *pasticceria* specializes in a creamy, thick bavarois cake, ricotta cheesecake, and rich chocolate profiterole cake.

A tour for those with a sweet tooth would not be complete without a visit to the Palazzo del Freddo di Giovanni Fassi, a large ice-cream parlor that has been in existence since the beginning of the twentieth century. On warm summer evenings, families congregate here to taste the *ninetto*, with its chocolate and cream flavor, or the Sicilian cassata, made with candied fruit. Their *semifreddo* selection is also first rate, especially with fruit or berries.

Agata e Romeo's restaurant has the merit of having been one of the first establishments in Rome to elevate the city's traditional recipes to haute cuisine. A cookery writer, teacher, and broadcaster as well as talented chef, Agata Parisella has a passion for recipes from the past, and her concern about contemporary cooking procedures, taste, and presentation has become a blueprint for many younger Roman chefs. From 1919, there has been an *osteria* on this site, where wine would be served only to those bringing their own hampers, the so-called *fagottari*. In later years Agata's father transformed it into a trattoria, a family-run establishment cooking simple fare. Agata eventually took up the family's business in 1980 with her husband, Romeo, a talented sommelier and the brains behind their impressive cellar, one of the best in Rome. Their daughter Maria Antonietta has also followed her parents' footsteps and selects their cheeses from producers across the whole of Italy.

A short walk from Agata and Romeo, past the bustle of the Termini railway station, is Trimani, a wine lovers' paradise with a selection of more than 5000 labels. The Trimani family's involvement with the wine trade dates back to 1821, when it sold wine from a small store in Via del Panico, near the Piazza Navona district. In 1876 they moved to the current premises of Via Goito, an area that was fast becoming the new district for the Roman bourgeoisie. Today the vast 400-square-meter space has a wine bar and spacious cellars. Among the original fittings are a Carrara marble top on the serving counter and, above it, a list of drinks from 1919 with lettering in gold leaf. The options – Vermouth, Marsala, and Ferro China – show what was popular in those times, as well as noting the cost for a glass: 40 cents in the old Italian lire.

Opposite: Esquilino patisserie Regoli has many sweet specialities – this is the *torta ai frutti di bosco*.

Pasta e broccoli in brodo di arzilla

Pasta and broccoli in skate broth

This classic tasty soup, traditionally served on Friday, the lean day of the week, combines pasta, vegetables, and skate. In the *romanesco* dialect, skate fish is called *arzilla*, apparently because of its lively character. Skate has a cartilage structure, which makes it perfect for creating a stock without bones.

piece of skinless skate, about 11 1/2 oz, halved crossways if
 large, rinsed
2 garlic cloves, chopped
1 celery stalk, roughly chopped
1 onion, peeled and left whole
extra-virgin olive oil
a few flat-leaf parsley leaves, chopped
1 red chili
1 anchovy filet (soak before using if heavily salted)
13 oz canned peeled tomatoes
2/3 cup dry white wine
7 oz romanesco or normal broccoli florets, cut into quarters
13 oz spaghetti, broken into short pieces
freshly squeezed lemon juice
salt

Put the skate in a large, heavy pot with enough salted water to cover. Boil for about 10 minutes. Add half the garlic, the celery stalk, and the onion. Season with salt. Remove the fish with a slotted spoon, allow it to cool and remove the cartilage with a serrated knife. Discard the cartilage and roughly chop the remaining flesh.

Return the fish chunks to the pot with the broth, and cook for another 3 minutes. Remove from the heat and set aside.

In another large pot, heat a little olive oil and gently fry the parsley, remaining garlic, chili, and anchovy. Add the tomatoes and wine, and sauté for 20 minutes. Add two ladles of the reserved skate stock, then the broccoli. Cook for 3 minutes. Add the remaining stock, bring to a boil and pour in the spaghetti. Cover and cook over a low heat for 5 minutes. Drizzle some olive oil and lemon juice over the soup before serving.

Terrine di coda alla vaccinara con puree di sedano e rapa

Oxtail terrine with celery and turnip purée

This recipe comes from Agata Parisello of the Agata e Romeo restaurant. Although very similar to the classic stewed oxtail recipe given in the Testaccio chapter, I have included it because it offers a more refined take on it. The oxtail is presented as a terrine on a bed of celery and turnip purée.

4 1/2 lb oxtail
4 tablespoons olive oil
4 white celery stalks, chopped
2 carrots, chopped
2 onions, chopped
2 or 3 bay leaves
1 tablespoon raisins
1 tablespoon pine nuts
2 cloves
1/2 cup dry white wine
1 lb 12 oz canned peeled tomatoes
2 teaspoons ground cinnamon
1 teaspoon bitter cocoa powder
2 turnips, chopped
olive oil
celery leaves (optional)
finely shredded deep-fried celery (optional)
salt and freshly ground black pepper

Follow the instructions given for coda alla vaccinara (see page 94), using three-quarters of the chopped celery and reserving the remainder for the purée. Towards the end of cooking, add the cocoa. Take the oxtail out of its sauce and scrape the meat from the bones. Discard the bones, and put the meat and its sauce in a 6 x 5 in terrine. Chill for 2 hours until set.

To make the purée, gently fry the celery and turnip with a little olive oil until golden. Remove from the pan, drain on paper towels and allow to cool. Purée in a liquidizer or food processor until smooth. Serve the purée at room temperature in a puddle on the plate, with a slice of terrine on top. If you wish, add a few celery leaves and deep-fried celery shreds as a garnish.

Millefoglie al cucchiaio

Millefoglie is the Italian version of the French pastry *mille feuille* (meaning "a thousand leaves") and is layered with Chantilly cream. In recent years it has become an incredibly popular dessert found in many top Roman restaurants. Everyone has their version. Agata Parisella, whose recipe is given here, piles it high as a column decorated with bitter chocolate, while the nearby Regoli pasticceria bakes it into a five-point star (see page 82).

You could use frozen puff pastry but if you have time, try to make the pastry yourself – it will have a lighter and more crumbly consistency. It is best to use Italian type 00 flour, widely available in supermarkets and Italian delicatessens. It is highly refined and has a lower level of gluten. It is important to work the pastry with cold ingredients and in a cool kitchen.

For the millefoglie pastry
2 1/4 cups flour (type 00)
1 teaspoon salt
1/2 teaspoon freshly squeezed lemon juice, strained
2/3 cup iced water to mix
2 5/8 stick chilled unsalted butter
confectioners' sugar for dusting

For the Chantilly cream
2 1/8 cups milk
1/4 teaspoon salt
1 vanilla pod, split lengthways
3 egg yolks
3/8 cup sugar
1/4 cup type 00 flour
2 1/8 cups heavy cream

To decorate
2 oz dark bitter chocolate, melted
2 tablespoons slivered almonds, toasted
1 tablespoon confectioners' sugar

To make the pastry, sift the flour and salt into a bowl. Tip onto a cool work surface, and make a well in the center. Pour the lemon juice into the well, mixing with just enough of the iced water to form a dough. Turn the dough onto a floured slab or board, and knead until smooth. Roll out to a 14 in square. Place the butter in the center and fold the pastry over it, sealing the edges well with a rolling pin. Flour the slab again and press the pastry out a little using the rolling pin, rolling into a long strip. Be careful not to let the butter break through the pastry. Flour the pastry lightly and fold it exactly in three, turning one fold away from you towards the center, then bringing the other edge towards you, so that the edge lies on the fold of the first piece of pastry. Again flour the slab, turn the fold to the left-hand side, gently roll out the pastry and fold in three. Place in the refrigerator for 10–15 minutes.

Remove from the refrigerator and again turn the fold to the left-hand side and roll out into a thin strip. Repeat the roll and fold procedure seven times, taking care to leave the pastry in the refrigerator for 10 minutes after every second roll. After the last roll, it should be left in the refrigerator for a further 25 minutes. It can then be rolled out and transferred to the baking sheet. Prick all over with a fork, and bake in a preheated oven at 350°F for about 15 minutes, or until the pastry is puffed and golden. Dust with confectioners' sugar and bake for another 5 minutes. Allow to cool on baking sheet. Cut some of the pastry into 3 in squares and break some into small shards.

To make the Chantilly cream, pour the milk into a pan, add the salt and vanilla pod, and bring slowly to the boil. In a bowl, whisk by hand the egg yolks, sugar, and flour with 1 tablespoon of the boiling milk. Add to the hot milk and continue whisking until free of lumps. Bring the custard to a boil over a moderate heat. Remove the pan from the heat and leave to cool. Lift out the vanilla pod and scrape the seeds into the milk. Transfer the custard to a bowl and chill in the refrigerator for at least 1 hour. Beat the heavy cream until it stands up in soft peaks. Carefully fold into the chilled custard.

To serve, place a generous tablespoon of Chantilly cream on the center of each individual dessert plate, then top with a pastry square, add another tablespoon of Chantilly cream, and another pastry square on top of that. Finally, top with pastry shards. Sift the confectioners' sugar over the top, drizzle with a little bit of melted chocolate and scatter with the almonds. Serve immediately.

Testaccio

Just across the southern end of the river Tiber, in front of the classy neighborhood of the Aventine hill, lies Testaccio, a lively, working-class area full of clubs, restaurants, food stores, and one of the noisiest food markets in the city. Since its beginnings as the river port of Rome, the area of Testaccio has always had an association with food. The very name derives from the Latin word *testum*, meaning amphorae or terracotta fragment. In ancient Roman times, Spanish olive oil was imported and transferred into smaller containers more apt for transportation. Once empty, the larger urns, drenched in oil, would be destroyed and thrown into a heap, set aside from the port. Over the years the debris formed a small hill, Il Monte dei Cocci (the mount of fragments). Eventually, grottoes were dug and used as stores by several artisans, as well as cellars for vegetables, oil, and wine.

Those who know Testaccio will tell you that by day it hasn't changed much. The covered fruit and vegetable market is still much cheaper than Campo dei Fiori, and its layout is less pretentious and pretty. Fishmongers bellow their daily offerings with pitched voices, while housewives rummage in the shoe stall selling fashion labels at half price. Many of the older restaurants that still serve local fare are called after the first names of their owners. Yet it is by night that Testaccio succumbs to the invasion of the modern era due to a maze of clubs, restaurants, and bars in and around the grottoes of the Monte dei Cocci, now known as "Testaccio village." As the young generation descends into the area, traffic is chaos and noise levels rise. In the summer, the grounds of the now disused slaughterhouse are packed for open-air concerts and the odd gay or reggae festival.

Even if the influx of writers, actors, and young students has changed the scene, Testaccio still manages to cling to its proletarian roots. A working-class culture was defined when Testaccio became the setting for the municipal slaughterhouse in 1890. Although closed down in 1973, its influence on the area remains. The slaughterhouse came to define the cuisine of Testaccio, which is not for the fainthearted, let alone vegetarians. The spiritual home of Roman meat eaters, Testaccio's restaurants specialize in serving succulent dishes the ingredients of which read like the anatomy of a cow. The blueprint of Roman cuisine was forged here at the door of the slaughterhouse, using both prime cuts of meat and the remaining offal. As a top-up to their wages, slaughterhouse workers used to be paid in *quinto quarto* (the fifth quarter) – the quarter of the carcass that

Opposite: The Roman tradition of *quinto quarto* cooking, made with the offal and those parts of the beast that were left over after the prime cuts of meat, was born here at the gates of the old Municipal slaughterhouse of Testaccio.

Food lovers' address book

Volpetti (gourmet shop)
Via Marmorata 47
tel +39 06 5742352
(www.volpetti.com for
deliveries worldwide)

Volpetti (bar/restaurant)
Via Volta 8
tel +39 06 5744305

Mercato di Testaccio
(food market)
Piazza Testaccio

Checchino dal 1887 (restaurant)
Via Monte Testaccio 30
tel +39 06 5743816

Agustarello (restaurant)
Via Branca 98
tel +39 06 5746585

Felice (restaurant)
Via Mastro Giorgio 29
tel +39 06 5746800

includes inner organs, head, tail and hooves. The total weight of this quarter that nobody wanted because it spoiled quickly was equivalent to a quarter of the slaughtered animal's weight, hence its name. Originally the workers would bring their quinto quarto payments to the restaurants nearby and have them cooked. This is how recipes such as *rigatoni alla pajata* (pasta with milk-fed veal, kid, or lamb intestines), *coda alla vaccinara* (braised oxtail) and *trippa alla romana* (slow-cooked tripe with tomato sauce) were born. While in other parts of the city today most Testaccio dishes may have been adapted and refined by restaurants, this is where to come to find the original and the authentic.

One of the most renowned establishments in Testaccio is Checchino, founded in 1887 when Lorenzo and Clorinda Moricci decided to convert their wine store in the caves of Monte Testaccio into a restaurant. Legend has it that it was the couple's daughter Ferminia Moricci who patented the Roman classic coda alla vaccinara recipe, braising it for seven hours in tomato sauce, celery, pine nuts, raisins, and bittersweet cocoa, and serving it the day after. Her son, Francesco, otherwise called Checchino, restored the restaurant in 1927 and turned it into a destination for politicians, businessmen, and artists, who were attracted by the gutsy, simple cuisine. Only one son of Checchino, Sergio, decided to follow his father's footsteps, and with his wife, Ninetta, he expanded the wine cellar to include many French labels as well those of Lazio. The restaurant's cellar is worth a visit alone, as it is the only one surviving inside the Monte dei Cocci, with visible fragments of terracotta still visible among the bricks. Due to the natural humidity, the wine's temperature can be kept acclimatized constantly both in the summer and in the winter. Today Sergio's sons Elio and Francesco Mariani run the restaurant with pride and expertise. Checchino methods of cooking have changed slightly since its inception, with olive oil substituting suet in the frying for example and certain cuts of meat being omitted due to BSE scares. Despite this, many recipes remain as deliciously authentic as a hundred years ago, and adventurous carnivores can sample salads of veal hoof, heart, lung, and esophagus of lamb cooked with artichokes, and fried sheep's brains.

Near the market is Felice a Testaccio, a typical trattoria run by the mercurial 83-year-old Felice. Every morning Felice goes to the market to buy the ingredients and, although he has many helpers in the kitchen, he insists on cooking the *carciofi alla romana* himself. Adored by Oscar-winning actor

Roberto Benigni, who once wrote a poem in his honor, Felice has built an establishment that is celebrated as *the* place to taste succulent suckling lamb, known as *abbacchio* in Rome. Beware, however, of his mood swings, and remember to eat all the contents of your dish – otherwise Felice might well decide you are not worthy of a second course. Felice is pure Roman spirit, clearly oblivious to the rules of courtesy, but excused by his patrons because of the excellent cuisine on offer.

Another celebrated Testaccio institution is Volpetti, a delicatessen stuffed with cheeses, salamis, breads, cakes, pasta, and ready-made dishes. Owners Claudio and Emilio Volpetti have run the place since 1973, transforming it, as the clientele itself changed and became more refined, into a gourmet pilgrimage site. In the past century, the shop was owned by a farmer who used to pasture his sheep in the fields nearby and sell the resulting fresh ricotta cheese on-site. It eventually graduated into a hat store, selling *le pagliette* (typical straw hats worn by Roman men), then into a *norcineria*, selling pork. The Volpetti family themselves are from nearby Norcia, a small hamlet called Località Case Volpetti, and from a long line of butchers and cheese makers. The store sells produce from all over Italy and prides itself on specializing in its stock of several types of ham, such as *prosciutto di Norcia*, Parma and *San Daniele di montagna*, as well as Parmesan cheese, buffalo mozzarella, and goat's cheese. Their pecorino romano comes from sheep grazing the neighboring countryside of Rome, and the local breads are delivered daily – although on Tuesdays and Fridays one can taste a delicious bread from Altamura in the Puglia region. A multicolored selection of *rustici* (the Roman savory cake) with stuffings such as *scarola* (a type of chicory), olives and capers, assorted cheeses, ricotta, and spinach are perfect as takeaway snacks. A visit just before Easter reveals an assortment of *torte pasqualine*, the cake traditionally eaten on Easter morning with boiled eggs and ham or *corallina*, a salami stuffed with lard and lean pork meat. On the shelves are *pizza ricresciuta al formaggio*, a savory bread-like cake made with pecorino; *casatiello tipo napoletano*, stuffed with pecorino, suet, salami, and sometimes boiled eggs; *torta pasqualina*, filled with ricotta, boiled eggs, and chard; and even the *pizza di Civitavecchia*, a traditional sweet cake from the seaside town of Civitavecchia made with ricotta, spices, and anise seed. Their delicious spelt cake, *torta di farro*, is a take on the Neapolitan Easter cake, *la pastiera napoletana*, traditionally made with whole grains and orange water.

Around the corner from the store, the Volpetti family have also opened a small cafeteria, serving quick lunches to locals and tourists alike. Behind the counters a tiny kitchen cum bakery churns out the pizzas and *torte rustiche*. *Fritti misti*, stuffed pizzas, and pasta dishes are all prepared using the first-class ingredients from the delicatessen.

Trippa alla Romana
Roman-style tripe

Chewy honeycomb tripe might not appeal to the squeamish, but once it is slow-cooked in a rich tomato sauce with a generous dose of Parmesan or pecorino cheese it becomes an irresistible, delicious main dish. Family-run Roman trattorie traditionally serve tripe on a Saturday, topped with a few mint leaves. Tripe can be made up to 2 days ahead and reheated just before serving.

2 1/4 lb honeycomb tripe, rinsed under cold
   running water
2 tablespoons extra-virgin olive oil
1 onion, chopped
2 garlic cloves, chopped
1 carrot, chopped
1 celery stalk, chopped
3 1/2 oz ham fat, roughly chopped
2/3 cup dry white wine
1 lb 12 oz canned peeled tomatoes
2 tablespoons tomato passata
a few mint leaves, chopped
3 1/2 oz pecorino or Parmesan cheese, grated
salt and freshly ground black pepper

Soak the tripe in a large bowl of cold water for 1 hour, then rinse under cold running water. Cut away any fat and discard. Bring a large pot of water to a boil. Add the tripe, bring back to a boil, then drain and rinse. Fill the pot with fresh water and bring the tripe to a boil again. Reduce the heat and simmer until tender – up to 4 hours.

   Drain the tripe in a colander and transfer to a cutting board. Cut into 2 in thick strips. Heat the olive oil in a large pot over a medium heat. Add the onion, garlic, carrot, celery, and ham fat, and gently fry for a few minutes. Add the tripe and the wine, bring to a boil and cook for 3 minutes. Season with salt and pepper, then reduce the heat to a simmer.

   Pour in the tomato and tomato passata, and bring the stew to boil. Add a few mint leaves. Then lower the heat and simmer for about 30 minutes, stirring the tripe until tender but still slightly chewy. Serve piping hot with a hefty dose of pecorino or Parmesan cheese on top.

Coda alla vaccinara
Oxtail stew

A staple of Roman gutsy cuisine, *coda alla vaccinara* is a great example of how to transform a "poor" cuisine plate into a palatable dish. This recipe is from Aldo Trabalza at Sora Lella.

4 tablespoons olive oil
4 1/2 lb oxtail or veal tail, fat removed, cut into
   sections
2 white celery stalks, chopped, plus 1 extra, cut into 1 in
   pieces
2 carrots, chopped
2 onions, chopped
2 or 3 bay leaves
1 tablespoon raisins
1 tablespoon pine nuts
2 cloves
1/2 cup dry white wine
1 lb 12 oz canned peeled tomatoes
2 teaspoons ground cinnamon
salt and freshly ground black pepper

Heat the olive oil in a large pot over a medium-high heat and add the oxtail. Gently fry, then stir in the chopped celery, carrots, onions, and bay leaves. Season with salt and pepper. Meanwhile, place the reserved celery in cold water. When the oxtail has browned slightly, stir in the raisins, pine nuts, and cloves, then add the wine. Cover and bring to a boil, then take the lid off and allow the wine to evaporate. Add the tomatoes and enough water to cover. Bring to a boil again, then turn the heat as low as possible. Stir in the cinnamon. Cook for about 2 hours. Add the extra celery strips and remove the cloves. Cook for another 40 minutes.

   Constantly check the consistency of the meat – it can sometimes be incredibly tender and need less cooking. In this case, transfer the meat to a plate. Keep simmering the sauce until condensed. Once ready, pour the sauce over the meat and serve. If the meat is tough, keep adding water to the pot to make it tender. Allow the meat to rest for 5–10 minutes before serving.

Saltimbocca alla romana
Roman-style veal escalopes

A dish now found everywhere in Italy and abroad, *saltimbocca* means that the meat is so good that it "jumps in your mouth." The recipe is very similar in execution to *involtini alla romana* (see Grottaferrata chapter, page 121), but the taste is very different. This recipe comes from the Checchino restaurant.

8 slices veal, about 1 lb
3 oz Parma ham, sliced
sage leaves – at least a leaf for each veal slice
flour for dusting
3 1/2 tablespoons butter
2/3 cup dry white wine
salt and freshly ground black pepper

Lay the veal slices flat on a clean work surface, and pound into thin escalopes. Place half a slice of the ham and a sage leaf in the middle of each escalope, then fold the escalope around its stuffing and hold in place with one or two toothpicks. Dust lightly with flour.

Melt the butter in a frying pan or skillet over high heat before adding the veal. Cook on both sides, then add the wine and allow it to evaporate. Reduce the heat, cover the pan with a lid and keep simmering for a few minutes. Turn off the heat and keep the lid on the pan until ready to serve.

Stracciatella

Stracciatella is a quintessential Roman soup. Its name comes from the way that the eggs used in the soup look like *straccetti* (little rags). The secret to preparing this soup is to stir the eggs in very quickly so that they shred finely.

Serves 6

3 eggs, beaten
freshly grated Parmesan cheese
pinch of ground nutmeg
8 1/2 cups cold chicken broth
1 tablespoon semolina or fine dry breadcrumbs (optional)
juice of 1/2 lemon
salt and freshly ground black pepper

Mix the eggs with about 2 tablespoons of grated Parmesan, nutmeg, a pinch of salt, pepper, and 1 tablespoon of the cold broth. Mix in the semolina or breadcrumbs, if using.

Bring the rest of the broth to a boil, then reduce the heat to a low simmer. Pour the egg mixture into the broth and whisk quickly until it sets and takes on the appearance of shredded strips of rag. Bring the broth back to a boil for a few minutes, then stir in the lemon juice. Serve immediately in warm bowls and sprinkle with a little Parmesan.

Fave fresche con guanciale

This is a simple *contorno*, which is what Romans call their vegetable side dishes. It makes use of the fresh fava beans that arrive in the market in spring and Roman *guanciale*, which can be successfully substituted with pancetta.

Serves 4

7 oz guanciale or pancetta, cubed
1 onion, sliced
a little olive oil
4 1/2 lb fresh fava beans still in their pods, or 1 1/4 lb shelled
1/2 cup dry white wine
salt and freshly ground black pepper

Heat a pan slightly and fry the cubed guanciale or pancetta and onion with a bit of olive oil. Add the fava beans and cook until they turn slightly golden. Add the wine, season with salt and pepper, and continue cooking, covered, for another 15 minutes.

Ricotta condita
Ricotta dessert

A yummy, super-fast dessert to make. When I was a child, I would mix the freshly made ricotta with some cocoa powder and sugar, pat it into a little ball, and eat it then and there, licking my spoon afterwards. A slightly more adult take on this is to mix it with egg yolks, sugar, and some liqueur.

13 oz fresh ricotta
2 tablespoons bitter cocoa powder
1/2 cup superfine sugar
3 egg yolks, beaten (optional)
2 tablespoons rum, Cognac, or Marsala (optional)
wafer cookies to serve

Combine all the ingredients and mix thoroughly. Pour the ricotta mixture into a mold or tall dessert glasses, and leave in the refrigerator for to chill for at least 1 hour. Serve with a wafer cookie. This is perfect accompanied by a glass of chilled white Fontana Candida or Malvasia.

R. XIV
BORGO PIO

Salame

Salami *Langhe*

Salame

ROMANESCHI
€ 0,35

prati
e borgo
pio

Prati e Borgo Pio

The fortified castle Castel Sant'Angelo, originally Adrian's Mausoleum, marks the beginning of the Borgo Pio and Prati area. The small village of Borgo Pio sprung up in AD 500, next to the Vatican just underneath the Leonina walls, hence the name Leonina city. Today Borgo Pio still has the slow pace of a small borough, away from the hustle and bustle of Rome's daily life. Its cobblestone streets are pedestrianized, and the medieval palazzi, covered in vine trellises and bougainvillea, make way for squares filled with the outdoor tables of local restaurants. The proximity to cultural stops such as the Sistine Chapel and the Vatican museums mean that the tourist trade is never far away, yet it is still possible to find establishments that feel authentic and local. Latteria Giuliani is possibly one of the last of Rome's remaining *latterie*, bars where one would come and buy the fresh dairy produce from local farms. Today it remains a social meeting point, where the elderly meet for a gossip, while the younger generation sip cappuccino.

Beyond Borgo lies Prati, a gentrified area that was originally called Prati di Castello ("fields of the castle") and largely used for recreation purposes. Prati is a wealthy suburb, built after the unification of Italy in 1870, and is characterized by a rational grid of housing blocks. Today the area is largely populated by the affluent Roman bourgeoisie and people working in the nearby studios of Italy's state-run television and radio stations. Media types abound, and it is quite common to bump into celebrities lining up at crowded restaurants on their lunch break. A typical Prati custom is to meet at chic bars Antonini or Vanni to sample the *tartine*, tiny, freshly made bread buns filled with caviar, smoked salmon, or crab. A dash of lemon juice is all that is needed before gulping down the delicacy, which is often served with an aperitif.

The food stores in Prati are as distinguished as the location demands. Enter Franchi and you will be faced with the staff clad in dinner jackets, as if ready for a summer ball, slicing sweet Parma ham or serving a portion of warm rice croquettes. Castroni next door is a temple to international gastronomy, and one of the first stores in Rome to sell exotic spices mixed with Italian cakes and pastries. Further on, in Via de Gracchi, a small residential courtyard leads to Tavola con lo Chef, arguably Rome's best cooking school. Here chefs such as Salvatore Tassa of Colline Ciociare (see Acuto chapter, page 124) and Nazareno Menghini from the restaurant in the Hotel de Russie share their secrets and offer short- or long-term courses to the dilettante or those aspiring to become professional cooks alike.

Every area of Rome has its district food market. Prati has a covered one in Piazza dell'Unità. Yet one of

Above: The imposing red-brick entrance to Borgo Pio, a small area next door to the Vatican that still retains the original flavor of a medieval borough. The local cafés, family-run trattorias and latterie selling dairy products are always buzzing with locals.

Rome's unsung food locations is the alternative market in Via Trionfale, which is large and always buzzing. Prices here are good and the selection of stalls is vast. The perimeter of the market is lined with stores called *alimentari* selling cheese, ham, and dried goods. The fruit and vegetable stalls, however, are the core of the market. Most stallholders are producers who work only from May to September when seasonal fruits such as strawberries, peaches, apricots, cherries, and figs emerge. Some of the stalls specialize in harder-to-find delicacies, such as wild mushrooms and asparagus. Towards the end of the market, near Via Caracciolo, the fish stalls sell mounds of silvery anchovies, stripey red mullet, snake-like eels, and *lattarini*, the tiny freshwater fish found in the waters of nearby Lake Bolzena.

Not far from the market is La Tradizione di Belli e Fantucci, a gourmet store selling more than 500 kinds of cheese, bought directly from small producers across Italy or seasoned in the shop's own caves in Val Nerina in Tuscany. From the caciocavallo cheese seasoned in oak barrels with mountain herbs to pecorino cheese with nuts, or ricotta cheese seasoned in hay, this is a paradise for discerning shoppers. The ham selection is also incredibly vast, with delicacies such as mule meat from the Vincentino area of North Italy, sweet Norcia ham, Milano salami, and *porchetta* ham from the Lazio town of Ariccia. For a potted history of each ingredient, owner Renzo Fantucci is on hand, to dispense anecdotes and courteous service as he has done for the past 20 years.

Back towards the Vatican is an unassuming restaurant called Dino and Tony which strives to guarantee a fun evening out. Two brothers originally from Amatrice, Dino and Tony have been in the restaurant trade since they were teenagers and are as quick in their service as they are with their wit. Their parents still live in Amatrice and it is in their cellar that Dino and Tony season the *guanciale* for their famed *pasta alla matriciana*. Dino and Tony serve all the classics of Roman cuisine and have a tendency for filling customers' tables with an array of antipasti. Generous portions of pizza, fried artichokes, olive *ascolane* (stuffed with meat), hams, and salami. However delicious their starter is, my advice is to forego it in favor of their excellent, simple *primi piatti*, which rival those of Prati's more illustrious establishments.

top to bottom: Students at the cookery school *A Tavola con lo Chef* in Via dei Gracchi, which runs courses for professionals as well as enthusiastic amateurs; Many locals find that the quickest way to negotiate Rome's busy streets is by Vespa; The colorful magazine stalls add an international flavor to Rome; Priests taking a stroll through the cobbled streets of Borgo Pio.

La Matriciana

Matriciana pasta sauce

La Matriciana is a dish originally created in Amatrice, a town north of Rome and, according to Dino at Dino and Tony, it started as a white sauce (see *tonnarelli alla gricia* on page 73) until the Bourbon kings conquered the area and "corrected" it with tomatoes. Whatever its origins, the sauce has always been a favorite of Romans, who, in their dialect, knocked off the "A" so that the name became *matriciana*. The most favored pasta shapes for this sauce are rigatoni, spaghetti, or bucatini. The crucial element is the *guanciale* (cured pork jowl). It is not easily found outside Italy, but can be substituted with good-quality bacon or pancetta.

5 oz guanciale or pancetta, thinly sliced and chopped
3 tablespoons olive oil
1 red chili, deseeded and shredded, or some chili flakes
2/3 cup dry white wine
13 oz canned peeled plum tomatoes
1 lb rigatoni, spaghetti, or bucatini
pecorino or Parmesan cheese

Bring a large pot of salted water to a boil. Fry the guanciale in a pan with the olive oil and the chili. As soon as the guanciale starts to color, pour in the wine, and allow to evaporate. Now pour in the tomatoes and allow to simmer until the sauce has reduced.

Add the pasta to the water and cook until al dente. Quickly drain and transfer immediately to the bubbling sauce. Stir for about 1 minute, then serve hot.

Pasta e ceci

Pasta and chickpeas

Roman cuisine makes an abundant use of legumes such as lentils, peas, chickpeas (garbanzo beans), borlotti beans, and fava beans. Combined with pasta or rice, they make filling, satisfying soups. This is a soup every Roman mamma traditionally cooks for her family on Tuesday, which along with Friday is considered a canonical "lean" day, a day during which one should not eat meat.

7 oz dried or 13 oz canned chickpeas (garbanzo beans)
1 sprig of rosemary
olive oil
3 garlic cloves, peeled and left whole
2 anchovy filets (optional), rinsed under running water to reduce salt, chopped
4 or 5 tomatoes, peeled and chopped
10 oz small pasta shapes such as cannolicchi, conchiglie, broken spaghetti, or quadrucci
freshly grated Parmesan cheese
salt and freshly ground black pepper

If using dried chickpeas, soak overnight in plenty of cold water with a pinch of bicarbonate of soda, changing the water often. If using canned chickpeas, simply rinse thoroughly and drain.

In a large pot, gently fry the rosemary sprig in a little olive oil with the garlic, the anchovies if using, the tomatoes and the chickpeas, until slightly colored. Add enough water to fill two-thirds of the pot, bring to a boil and season with salt. Add the pasta, adding more water if necessary, and cook until al dente.

Serve the soup hot drizzled with a little olive oil, seasoned with pepper and with some freshly grated Parmesan sprinkled over the top.

Fettuccine con il ragù

Fettuccine with meat sauce

A simple Italian recipe from the lessons given
by Salvatore Tassa (see page 124). The coarse
consistency of homemade fettuccine works well
with the rich tomato and meat sauce

Serves 4–6

For the fettucine
4 cups (1 lb) Italian type 00 flour
6 eggs

For the ragù
2 tablespoons extra-virgin olive oil
1 1/2 tablespoons butter
1 small carrot, finely chopped
1 small celery stalk, finely chopped
1/2 onion, finely chopped
10 oz ground beef
3 tablespoons red wine
**7 oz canned peeled tomatoes or fresh plum tomatoes, peeled
  and deseeded**
2 1/2 tablespoons tomato purée (paste)
4 1/4 cups beef stock
salt and freshly ground black pepper

To make the pasta, pile the flour in the center of a clean
work surface, making a well in the middle. Put the eggs in
the well, stirring in the flour from the edges and gradually
kneading together until you obtain a smooth, rubbery
dough. Wrap in plastic wrap and leave to rest for at least
30 minutes.

Divide the dough into five balls and roll them out into
rectangles that can pass through a pasta machine. Set
the machine to its widest setting. Fold a sheet of dough
into the machine at least twice. Change it to a narrower
setting, then fold the dough and pass again through the
machine. Keep folding the dough into the machine until
you reach the narrowest setting for fettuccine. The
pastry should be translucent but of a consistency thick
enough not to tear. Repeat with the remaining dough.

To cut the pasta, attach the fettuccine cutter and pass
the sheet of dough through the cutter. Once cut, gather
a few strands and curl them into small nests. Leave to
dry on clean tea towels.

To make the ragù, put the olive oil and butter in a
frying pan with the carrot, celery and onion. Gently fry
for a few minutes, and before the onion starts to color,
turn the heat to medium-high and add the ground beef.
Stir, letting the meat brown slightly before adding the wine
and allowing it to evaporate. Next add the tomatoes
and season with salt and pepper. Add the tomato
purée (paste) and the stock. Simmer over a low heat
for 1 1/2 hours, adding some more stock if necessary. The
final sauce should be thick and concentrated.

Cook the fettucine in plenty of boiling salted water until
al dente – as the pasta is fresh you will only need to cook
it for about 4 minutes. Drain quickly and serve on plates
with the sauce spooned over the top.

Seppie e carciofi
Squid and artichokes

For many years this was one of the few seafood dishes one would find on Rome's restaurant menus. Luckily, since the advent of institutions such as La Rosetta (see page 36), Romans have become a little more adventurous in their fish and seafood choices, and well versed in eating practically everything from sea bass to sushi. However, this particular dish remains a firm favorite of trattorie and home cooking. Squid can also be cooked with peas.

1 1/4 lb ready-cleaned squid
2 garlic cloves
a little olive oil
1 fresh red chili, deseeded and chopped
2/3 cup dry white wine
13 oz canned peeled tomatoes or 4 plum tomatoes, peeled and deseeded
2 or 3 globe artichokes, cleaned and sliced (see page 62)

Wash and pat the squid dry with paper towels. Cut the main body into large chunks and mince the tentacles.

Gently fry the garlic in a pan with olive oil, then add the chili and the squid. Pour in the wine and let it evaporate, then add the tomatoes. Increase the heat to medium and bring the squid mixture to a boil. After 10 minutes, reduce the heat and add the artichoke. Cook for another 15 minutes until tender. Serve hot.

Tiramisù
Tiramisu

This iconic Italian dessert's reputation has been tarnished by the many mediocre versions served around the world over the years. When made with top-notch, fresh ingredients, however, it becomes a light and creamy dessert, ideal for dinner parties.

Serves 4–6

3 eggs, separated
1/2 cup granulated sugar
1 lb mascarpone cheese
2 tablespoons Marsala
4 tablespoons grated bitter chocolate
18 biscotti di savoiardi (ladyfingers, or Savoy biscuits) or 8 oz sponge cake
1 1/2 cups freshly brewed coffee

Whisk the egg yolks with the sugar until thick and pale. Fold in the mascarpone. Beat the egg whites in a separate bowl until they form stiff peaks. Add the Marsala and 2 tablespoons of the grated chocolate. Whisk again until the egg mixture now forms soft peaks. Fold it gently into the mascarpone mixture.

Place a layer of cookies in the bottom of a deep glass baking dish. Pour half the coffee over the top, making sure the cookies are well soaked. Spread half of the mascarpone mixture evenly over the cookies. Make another layer using the remaining cookies, coffee, and mascarpone. Sprinkle with the remaining chocolate. Chill for at least for 4 hours before serving.

fra
scati

Frascati

There is nothing the Romans like better than a day trip beyond the city walls; hence the term *gita fuori porta* (literally "trip outside the wall"). Traditionally this would involve a picnic, filled with easy-to-make delicacies such as egg frittata, panzanella (dried bread revived by tomatoes), salty pecorino cheese, raw fava beans, and a bottle of Frascati wine. On Easter Monday, what the Romans call *pasquetta*, families take advantage of the mild spring climate and congregate in noisy crowds along the Via Appia Antica, choosing a sunny spot among the ancient ruins to enjoy a spread of leftovers from their Easter breakfast.

On May Day, Romans head south-west, towards the hilly region of the Castelli Romani and in particular to the town of Frascati to taste the local wines. Here one can still find the *frasche*, outdoor wine bars so called because a *fraschetta* (small tree branch) would be hung outside to mark the arrival of the new wine. Customers would bring their own *fagotti* (hampers of food) and overindulge in the chilled, honey-scented wine under the shade of the vineyard trellises.

The Frascati area has been a holiday resort since Roman times, when senators and emperors built villas to retreat to in order to escape the city's stifling summer heat. From 1559 onwards, the Frascati enjoyed a glorious period, with the Roman aristocratic families Aldobrandini, Lancellotti, Falconieri, Mondragone, Parisi, Muti, Grazioli, and Torlonia building grandiose palaces known as the Tuscolo villas, each one a physical expression of the hedonistic pursuits of the rich. Architecturally, severe-looking façades hide sumptuous frescoes and intricate landscaped gardens, representing the social divide between the aristocratic Romans and the inhabitants of the town.

Today social classes mix seamlessly in places such as the airy Cacciani restaurant, brought together by the love for good, simple food. Local families with small children and groups of Romans mix with the tourists and businessmen, here to enjoy the chattering buzz of this Frascati institution, a restaurant originally started in nearby Cinecittà in 1922 by Leopoldo Cacciani. In the 1950s the site moved to Frascati and is today run by the third-generation brothers Leopoldo and Paolo, and sister Caterina Cacciani. Starters such as *bruschetta alla provola* are revived by using a fragrant, home-baked bread with squid ink, while their *cacio e pepe* is blended with tomato. Only organic vegetables are used for their *fritto misto* (a mix of deep-fried vegetables) and local lambs for their *abbacchio scottadito* (so called because the suckling lamb is cooked so hot that it burns your fingers). The menu is strictly seasonal and still follows the rule of *giorni comandati*, the Catholic canonical calendar of days traditionally divided into lean and feast days. Whether a Sunday, a wedding, or a birthday, Cacciani is a restaurant for special occasions, and the atmosphere is always one of celebration.

Above: The gentle sloping hills situated around Frascati are the ideal habitat for vineyards. Picturesque and significantly quieter than the urban center of Rome, this area has been favored for centuries by Romans, who have used it as a backdrop for picnics, out of town trips, and fabulous hideaway villas.

Pappardelle al pesto frascatano
Pappardelle with Frascati pesto

This is Cacciani's variation of the Ligurian pesto sauce. Almonds substitute pine nuts, oregano is used instead of basil and a hefty does of ricotta gives it a true Roman flavor. To make your own pappardelle, use the fettucine recipe on page 108, but make the strips wider, 1 in ribbons.

1/4 lb new potatoes, diced
4 vine-ripened tomatoes, chopped
1 tablespoon crushed almonds
7 oz fresh ricotta
2 garlic cloves, chopped
bunch of oregano, leaves picked and chopped, plus extra
  for garnish
a little olive oil
13 oz pappardelle
freshly grated Parmesan or pecorino cheese
salt and freshly ground black pepper

Boil the potatoes for about 5 minutes until cooked but not mushy. In a serving bowl, mix the tomato, almonds, ricotta, garlic, oregano, and enough olive oil to moisten. Cook the pappardelle in boiling salted water until al dente. Use a ladleful of the cooking water to blend the pesto mixture together. Add the potatoes. Drain the pappardelle, add to the serving bowl and toss through. Sprinkle with Parmesan and freshly ground pepper. Garnish with oregano leaves.

Pollo alla romana
Roman-style chicken

This quintessential Roman dish has been around for ages, but, as always with tradition, everyone seems to have their own variation. Famed Roman writer and cook Ada Boni adds marjoram to it, while a popular variation is with red peppers. At Cacciani, *pollo alla romana* is listed as *un piatto della tradizione*, and those who order it are entitled to a special, somewhat kitsch-looking, hand-painted plate, decorated with a cockerel draped in a Roman toga. The secret to the recipe is to choose a free-range chicken, what Italians call *ruspante*, as its meat is much more flavorful and needs little preparation.

1 free-range or corn-fed chicken, about 3 lb, cut into 8 pieces
  (you can ask your butcher to do this)
olive oil
4 garlic cloves, crushed
small fistful of capers, desalted under cold, running water
pinch of dried oregano
1 1/2 cups dry white wine
1 lb 12 oz canned peeled tomatoes
1 red pepper, cored, deseeded, and sliced (optional)
salt and freshly ground black pepper

Gently fry the chicken pieces in a large deep pan in some olive oil. Add the garlic, capers, oregano, and salt and pepper to taste. Once the chicken has soaked up all the flavors, pour in the wine and allow it to evaporate. Add the tomatoes and continue cooking for about 30 minutes until the sauce has concentrated. Stir every now and then to prevent the chicken from sticking to the pan. When the meat has separated from the bones, the chicken is ready.

As a variation, you can add a few slices of red peppers if you wish and let them cook with the chicken for a further 15 minutes.

Zuppa inglese
Roman trifle

Zuppa inglese is a custard-laden and liqueur-sodden dessert the name of which (literally "English soup") is partially justified by a faint resemblance to trifle. It is called soup because it is so steeped in custard that it needs to be eaten with a spoon. One story dates its creation to around 200 years ago by the courts in the Frascati villas, to celebrate a visit from the Queen of England. Others say it was the Roman Aragno *pasticceria* in Via del Corso that came up with a recipe to satisfy its assiduous British customers.

Cacciani's version uses a glass of cherry Maraschino liqueur and half a glass of Alkermes Luxardo, a flowery and lightly spiced liqueur. Because Alkermes is hard to find, I have included as an alternative Marcella Hazan's combination of liqueurs, as outlined in *The Essentials of Classic Italian Cooking*. Cherry brandy, Marsala, or other types of aromatic liqueur work equally well.

The base of the cake is sponge cake or, if you can find them at an Italian delicatessen, *biscotti di savoiardi* (ladyfinger cookies).These cookies are of medieval origin and were prepared by chefs for the Dukes of Savoy when the kings visited France. They are widely used in Italian cakes and are the base for tiramisù.

For the custard
2 1/8 cups milk
1 vanilla pod, split lengthways
5/8 cup superfine sugar
grated zest of 1 lemon
1/2 cup flour
3 egg yolks

For the sponge layer
36 biscotti di savoiardi (ladyfinger cookies) or 1 lb sponge cake
4 tablespoons Alkermes Luxardo, or 8 tablespoons Marsala, or 1 tablespoon rum mixed with 2 tablespoons cognac and 2 tablespoons Drambuie
8 tablespoons Maraschino liqueur
4 tablespoons blackberry or cherry jam
2 tablespoons bitter cocoa powder

For the topping
2 oz dark (bittersweet) chocolate, melted
1 oz toasted almonds, chopped

To make the custard, pour the milk into a saucepan and add the vanilla pod, bringing the liquid slowly to a boil. Stir in half the sugar and the lemon zest. In a mixing bowl, whisk the flour with the remaining sugar, adding a tablespoon of the boiling milk and whisking continuously until lump-free. Whisk in the yolks, then pour into the saucepan of boiling milk, whisking energetically until the custard is thick. Remove the pan from the heat and allow to cool. Lift out the vanilla pod and scrape the seeds into the milk with the point of a small knife, discarding the pod. Chill the custard in the refrigerator for about 45 minutes.

Line a shallow bowl or glass dish with the savoiardi to create a base. Pour the Alkermes Luxardo over the base, making sure it is thoroughly soaked. Using a spatula, spread a layer of cooled custard about 1/2 in thick over the savoiardi. Spread 2 tablespoons of the jam on top. Cover with another layer of savoiardi and this time soak with Maraschino liqueur. Spread over another layer of custard, this time mixed with the cocoa powder, then add the remaining 2 tablespoons jam. Cover the top with the third and final layer of soaked savoiardi. Leave in the refrigerator to set for at least 1 hour. Serve topped with melted chocolate and a sprinkle of almonds.

grotta
ferr
ata

Grottaferrata

Sometimes a meal in an out-of-town restaurant is reason enough for a day trip. Favorite haunts are those where the atmosphere is informal, the service attentive, and the menu seasonal. La Briciola di Grottaferrata holds all the ingredients for an idyllic out-of-town restaurant. Strategically placed in Grottaferrata, just outside Frascati, it is on the route that leads to the volcanic lakes of Nemi and Albano, and the towns of Marino and Castelgandolfo, the site of the pope's summer villa. The town's main attraction is the fortified Abbey of Saint Nilo, named after the Greek orthodox saint who sought refuge from the Saracens in this area around 1004.

La Briciola's owner and cook Adriana Montellanico and her husband, Alberto Lombardi, are well versed in the art of charming their customers. If you are lucky, you might catch Alberto in a singing and entertaining mood, as he is an avid collector and connoisseur of American jazz and Italian music, and loves sharing anecdotes. Cooking is in Adriana's veins, as her family used to run a famous restaurant called Osteria Il Gladiatore (the gladiator) near the Coliseum in the 1930s, and her mother even won a gold medal with her recipe for *involtini alla romana* (see page 121). Adriana's alter ego in the kitchen is shy and retiring chef Fabio Cardia, with whom she rustles up specialities such as *zucchine alle velletrana* (zucchini cooked in the style of the nearby town of Velletri, for which she won't dispense the recipe), a crunchy pear and chocolate crumble, and of course, *la vignarola* and *abbacchio brodettato*.

Adriana is also a wonderful raconteur, and just hearing her explanations of the origin of the dishes on the menu is worth the visit alone. Each ingredient, from the *tagliolini* pasta freshly made by an old lady down the road to the wild fennel used in her bean soup, has a traceable origin and a story behind it. Customers here are made to feel welcome and part of a culture of eating and conviviality.

From La Briciola, the vineyards of Castel de Paolis are just a short drive away and should be visited, if only to meet the charming owner Giulio Santarelli. Only started in the mid 1990s, his vineyard is almost an oddity in the otherwise mostly quite bland scenario of Frascati regional wines. With the help of consultant Franco Bernabei, Santarelli has brought in grape varieties such as Viognier, which is the basis of his excellent white Vigna Adriana, named after his wife, and Syrah, Merlot, Petit Verdot, and Cabernet for his multiple award-winning Quattro Mori. In 2004, Castel de Paolis was awarded best organic wine producer, and its stature and reputation will no doubt continue to improve. Giulio has great plans for the coming years and is expanding his offices and cellars into tasting facilities and a concert hall overlooking the splendid vineyards.

Above: The fortified abbey of Grottaferrata attracts visitors worldwide, and the nearby restaurant, La Briciola, also has gourmets and gourmands coming back for more.

Food lovers' address book

La Briciola (restaurant)
Via Gabriele d'Annunzio 18
tel +39 06 9459338
Castel de Paolis
(wine producer)
Via Val de Paolis
tel +39 06 9413648
Cantina Colonna (restaurant)
Marino
Via G. Carissimi 32
tel +39 06 93660386

La Vignarola
Pea, artichoke, and fava bean stew

This is Adriana Montellanico's signature dish. Her trick is to cook the vegetables in different pots so that their individual flavors develop. She combines them in one pot just before serving.

1 globe artichoke
1 lemon, halved
olive oil
1 onion, chopped
2 3/4 cups water
10 oz shelled green peas
10 oz guanciale or pancetta (optional), sliced and finely chopped
pinch of freshly chopped chili
10 oz shelled fava beans
1 teaspoon sugar
1 garlic clove
a few mint leaves, coarsely chopped
1/2 cup dry white wine
freshly chopped flat-leaf parsley (optional)
salt and freshly ground black pepper

Clean the artichoke (see page 62), and slice into small sections. Rub with lemon to prevent blackening. Heat a little olive oil in a saucepan and gently fry half the onion. Season, then pour in half the water. When it boils, add the peas, then reduce the heat, and cover with a lid.

Meanwhile, in a second saucepan, gently fry the guanciale. Add the remaining onion and the chili, continue frying at a very low heat. Pour in the remaining water, increase the heat to high, and bring to a boil. Add the fava beans and sugar, and reduce the heat. Cover the pan with a lid and allow to simmer gently.

In a third saucepan, add 4 tablespoons of olive oil, the garlic, mint, wine, and a pinch of salt and pepper. Mix thoroughly then add the artichoke. Cover with baking parchment and a lid. Bring to a boil, then simmer for about 10 minutes until tender.

Transfer all the vegetables to one pan and cook for 10 minutes more. Add the parsley, if using, and serve in bowls with a little bit of olive oil drizzled over the top.

Involtini di manzo alla romana con piselli
Roman-style beef rolls with peas

This is a typical "poor" Roman dish, traditionally made with the *panicolo*, a cheap cut of beef derived from the lower stomach of the cow. To make the most of it, the meat would be butchered lengthways and stewed for several hours until it reached a soft consistency. To add flavor, scraps from prosciutto bones, and celery and carrots were added. Today it is cooked with thin-sliced beef and served with tender and sweet green peas.

8 thin slices boneless beef top round, about 13 oz
4 slices Parma ham, about 2 oz
2 carrots, cut into julienne
2 celery stalks, cut into julienne
4–6 basil leaves, torn in half
5 tablespoons olive oil
1 small onion, chopped
2 garlic cloves, peeled and left whole
1/2 cup dry white wine
1 1/4 lb canned peeled tomatoes
4 cloves
1 bay leaf
10 oz shelled green peas, fresh or frozen
salt and freshly ground black pepper

Lay the beef slices flat on a clean work surface. Pound into thin escalopes. Season with salt and pepper, and place half a slice of ham, a carrot stick, a celery stick, and a piece of basil in the middle of each slice of beef. Wrap the escalope around its stuffing and secure it in place with one or two toothpicks.

Heat the oil in a large frying pan and gently fry the beef. Add the onion, garlic, and the remaining celery and carrot, and fry for 2 minutes. Then add the wine, let it evaporate, and add the tomatoes, cloves, the remaining basil, and the bay leaf. Reduce the heat, cover the pan with a lid and cook for at least 1 hour.

Stir the peas into the pan and cook for a further 12 minutes. Remove the toothpicks, garlic, and cloves, and serve immediately.

Fragoline di Nemi con zabaglione
Wild strawberries with zabaglione cream

Nearby Nemi produces the most delicious wild strawberries in Lazio. Only available for a short season, their taste is a far cry from the larger farmed ones. Adriana simply places them on her homemade chilled zabaglione, creating a scrumptious dessert.

Zabaglione needs to be cooked in a double boiler – if you do not have a double boiler, use a smaller saucepan placed inside a large one.

4 egg yolks
1 1/2 tablespoons superfine sugar
1 1/2 tablespoons Marsala or sherry
wild strawberries or best-quality small, sweet strawberries

Combine the egg yolks with the sugar in the top half of a double boiler. Whip the mixture over hot but not boiling water, until the sauce coats the back of a spoon. Stir in the Marsala, then immediately pour the zabaglione into individual serving glasses.

Cover with plastic wrap and leave in the refrigerator to chill for 1 hour before serving. Add a generous amount of strawberries to each glass and serve.

Acuto

There is an area little known to foreign travelers just 45 miles south of Rome called Ciociaria. A mountainous and relatively unspoiled region, its only claim to international fame is the 1964 Vittorio de Sica film called *La Ciociara*, starring a youthful and unsophisticated Sophia Loren. Yet the region has all the ingredients to become a well-trodden tourist path. Dotted with small medieval towns, it is a fertile wine- and olive-growing region, full of small farms producing delicious produce such as ricotta cheese, ham, and *guanciale*.

Since 1973, this area is the only one near the city of Frosinone to boast the Italian DOC denomination on its red wines, produced from the indigenous varieties Cesanese and Affile. These once humble grapes have been turned into refined wines by producers such as Massimo Berucci, Perinelli, and Terenzi and Coletti Conti. The wine-growing area lies between the nearby towns of Anagni, Acuto, Serrone, Paliano, and Piglio.

Up a winding road among the olive groves is the small town of Acuto, originally the outpost of Anagni bishops and the top of which is crowned by a well-conserved medieval castle with cylindrical towers. But it is Salvatore Tassa's restaurant, Le Colline Ciociare, on the outskirts of Acuto, that is Lazio's best-known pilgrimage stop for enthusiastic foodies. A real oddity within the conventional Italian gastronomic scene, Salvatore is a self-taught cook who 15 years ago packed in his architecture job which took him round the world to convert his mother's trattoria into a gourmet destination. Over the years, the 1950s building has been lovingly restored to a Pompeii red, 1700s-style Neapolitan home. His great-grandmother's bedhead, featuring an oil painting of the Madonna of Pompeii, stands in the main living room; 1700s farmhouse tiles have been strategically placed as decorative elements; and an old chimney enshrined by a newly built white metal-roofed structure is a reminder of the brick production of the area.

Although born in Bradford in the UK, from where his parents had migrated in the 1950s and where they returned 10 years later, Salvatore is decidedly attached to his roots. All his dishes are based on local seasonal ingredients which he employs as a canvas for his innovative techniques. Sheep's milk ricotta, red and yellow onions, milk-fed lamb, parsnips, beets, and a generous use of herbs are staples of his cuisine, one that does not follow traditions nor trends, but is always impeccable in its quality. While Lazio may not be known for haute cuisine, it has achieved new heights with the skills of Salvatore Tassa.

Opposite: Away from the well-trodden tourist paths lies Ciociara, an area full of beautiful small towns like Acuto, wine producers, and small batch farmers. Just on the outskirts of Acuto is Salvatore Tassa's restaurant Le Colline Ciociare, arguably the best in Lazio.

La cipolla fondente
Roasted stuffed onions

This is Salvatore Tassa's signature dish, one that people travel for miles to eat. Its simplicity is astounding, and the final presentation is bound to impress even the most jaded guests. For those worried about ingesting a whole onion, let it be known that the cooking process allows the breakdown of all those acid substances that make onions hard to digest. You can serve it as a starter or appetizer with a glass of red Cesanese del Piglio.

1 lb coarse sea salt or Maldon sea salt flakes
4 large yellow onions, unpeeled
a little olive oil
freshly ground black pepper

Take a small baking tray and pour a thick layer of sea salt onto it. Place the onions on top and cover them completely with the rest of the salt. Bake in a preheated oven at 400°F for at least an hour. When cooked, remove the salt crust from the onions and trim off the tops.

Gently scoop out all the flesh of the onion, making sure you keep the shell intact. Blend the onion flesh in a food processor or liquidizer, or push through a sieve, until the consistency is smooth. Then season with a little bit of olive oil and salt.

Refill the onion shells with the onion purée. If serving immediately, put the onions back in the oven and bake for another 8–10 minutes. Otherwise keep the onions in the refrigerator and warm them just before serving. Serve one onion per head on a plate, seasoned with a little bit of olive oil and freshly ground pepper.

Food lovers' address book

Le Colline Ciociare (restaurant)
Via Prenestina 27 Acuto
tel +39 0775 56049

Cannoli croccanti di polenta

Polenta flour cannoli with ricotta cheese

This recipe plays with the conventional idea that *cannoli* are dessert stuffed with ricotta; however, Tassa's version is a delicious savory alternative to be served as a main course. If you cannot find polenta flour in an Italian delicatessen, try substituting it with plain white flour.

2 small globe artichokes, cleaned (see page 62)
squeeze of lemon juice
1 1/8 cups polenta flour
2 eggs
vegetable oil for frying
10 oz sheep's milk or other ricotta, sieved
a few marjoram and mint leaves
2 oz guanciale or pancetta, cut into small slivers
3 1/2 oz cooked red beets
2/3 cups vegetable stock
a little olive oil
2 garlic cloves, peeled and left whole
a few sprigs of thyme
salt and freshly ground black pepper

Cut the artichokes into thin slivers and place in a bowl of water with lemon juice to prevent blackening.

Make a dough with the flour, eggs, and a little salt. Roll out until paper thin. Cut into 8 squares and wrap them round metal baking cylinders. Deep-fry the cannoli until golden in a pan of piping-hot vegetable oil, then drain on paper towels. Gently remove the cylinders.

Season the ricotta with a little salt and pepper. Fill the cannoli with the ricotta and bake in a preheated oven at 325°F for about 10 minutes.

Deep-fry the artichokes with a few mint and marjoram leaves. Drain on absorbent kitchen paper. Fry the guanciale in a pan. Meanwhile, blend the beets with enough vegetable stock to make them liquid, then gently heat in a pan with a little oil, garlic, and thyme.

To serve, spoon a strip of beet sauce onto a plate. Place one of the cannoli beside it, then top with a small pile of artichokes and pancetta. Drizzle some olive oil on the plate, season with salt and pepper, and top with a mint sprig as a garnish.

Fettuccine al pomodori e menta

Fettuccine with oven-roasted tomatoes and mint

This is a variation of Salvatore Tassa's recipe made with ingredients readily available outside Italy. The trick is to slow-roast the tomatoes in the oven so that their juices are intensified. Home-made fettuccine (see recipe on page 108) adds rustic texture to the dish.

13 oz fresh or canned cherry tomatoes, halved
olive oil
pinch of sugar
10-12 mint leaves
a bit of crushed dried chili
1 lb home-made or store-bought fettucine
pecorino or Parmesan cheese
salt

Place the cherry tomatoes on a baking tray with a little bit of olive oil, a pinch of sugar and salt. Sprinkle some of the mint leaves on top. Bake in a preheated oven at 350°F for 20 minutes. When the tomatoes are ready, place them in a large serving bowl with all the juices and sprinkle the chili over them.

Meanwhile bring a large pot of salted water to the boil. Cook the fettucine until al dente. Drain, keeping a ladleful of the cooking water. Toss the fettuccine in the bowl with the tomato and the reserved cooking water. When all the ingredients are well blended, sprinkle some pecorino over the top and decorate with a few extra mint leaves. Serve immediately.

Ostia

Nothing beats a hot summer day spent on the *litorale romano*, the long stretch of sea punctuated by resorts such as Fregene, Maccarese, Torvajanica, and Castel Porziano. As with football teams, each seaside resort has its die-hard fans who religiously turn up at the same beach every year, idly tanning themselves all day long, only to take a break to eat seafood classics such as *spaghetti allo scoglio* (seafood spaghetti) or *trancio di pesce spada* (swordfish steak) for lunch. Unlike the more chic resort of Fregene, home to movie stars and intellectuals, Ostia was until very recently a run-down sea resort with a reputation for dirty beaches and uneventful restaurants. The only reason it stayed on the tourist map was the excavations of Ostia Antica, the ancient Roman town and river port built in AD II. The current location of the town of Ostia is pretty near to the original port, next to the Tiber's outlet into the Tyrrhenian Sea.

From 1916 a new regeneration plan saw Ostia being transformed into a "garden city," with large French-style boulevards and a rational grid. In the 1930s, Mussolini turned it into a "Rome at the sea" destination, building a whole series of Art Deco style buildings, which, with their large white- and pastel-colored blocks with portholes, sails, and other nautical references somewhat recall an Italian version of Miami. Over the years, the eighteenth-century villas and Fascist style beach resorts that line the seafront had slowly faded, largely out of neglect for its architectural heritage and because of Ostia's decline in popularity. Now, the shores are being cleaned up, the resorts are being slowly restored, and Ostia seems to be enjoying a renaissance.

Most importantly, a surprising seafood restaurant has set tongues wagging and has become a favorite destination for discerning day-trippers. The Rosario restaurant, named after its owner, whose family runs a renowned fish store, Rio Pesca in Rome, has become, in only five years, a prime location for creative seafood cooking. Much of the merit goes to the connection with Rio Pesca, which obviously guarantees the availability of top-quality fish on a daily basis. Above all, however, it is the talented chef Antonio Chiappini who deserves the most praise, as he has built a menu which is full of Mediterranean flavors cooked in the simplest way possible while being open to surprising combinations not conventionally found in your average *cucina marinara*. Located next to the 1922-built Salus resort, Rosario also benefits from a great outdoor terrace space that helps make the experience of eating outside on the sea-shore even more pleasurable.

Opposite: No day at the seaside could be complete without a hearty plate of spaghetti alle vongole, digested in the shade of a sun umbrella.

Food lovers' address book

Rosario (restaurant)
Lungomare Paolo
Toscanelli 119
tel +39 06 5612727

Totani fritti con purea di melanzane

Fried baby squid with eggplant mash and balsamic vinegar sauce

This might seem like adventurous recipe for a Roman seafood restaurant, yet its composition is very simple and filled with classic Mediterranean flavors. Chef Antonio Chiappini uses *totani*, small baby squid, which are the same type employed in Thai cuisine.

1 lb eggplants
juice of 1 lemon
4 tablespoons olive oil
1 garlic clove, chopped
3/8 cup balsamic vinegar
1 tablespoon soy sauce
2 lb baby squid, cleaned
1 1/2 cups flour
4 1/4 cups vegetable oil for cooking
salt and freshly ground black pepper

Prick the eggplants with a fork, place them on a baking sheet and bake in a preheated oven at 350°F for 30 minutes. Peel and chop them into cubes and purée them in a food processor or liquidizer, or push through a sieve with the lemon juice and 2 tablespoons of the olive oil until smooth.

Gently fry the garlic in the remaining 2 tablespoons olive oil. Add the balsamic vinegar and soy sauce. Continue cooking the sauce until reduced in volume by two-thirds.

With a small, sharp knife, make a cross on each baby squid. Dust with the flour and fry in a pan with sizzling vegetable oil. Drain well on paper towels. To serve, pour a tablespoon of eggplant purée onto a large plate, place the baby squid on top and drizzle the caramelized vinegar sauce over the top.

Tonno lardato con tartare di melone e salsa al porto allo scalogno

Tuna wrapped in lard with a melon tartare and port sauce

Chef Antonio Chiappini uses either cod or tuna for this dish, but I find that red seared tuna meat goes well with the crunchy sweet melon, both aesthetically and tastewise. The fish is wrapped in slices of *lardo di Colonnata*, a lard produced in the small town of Colonnata in Tuscany and an ingredient that is become increasingly fashionable in Italian cuisine. It can still be difficult to find outside Italy, and I would avoid substituting it with normal types of lard. If you cannot find it, simply don't use lard at all – the fresh zestiness of this dish also works well without it.

4 small filets tuna , about 1 1/4 lb
8 slices lardo di Colonnata
13 oz sweet melon, such as cantaloupe, roughly chopped into cubes
juice of 1/2 lemon
1/2 shallot, chopped
1 tablespoon extra-virgin olive oil
scant 1/2 cup port
scant 1/2 cup balsamic vinegar
3 1/2 tablespoons clear honey
a few cherry tomatoes, halved (optional)
baby spinach leaves (optional)
salt and freshly ground black pepper

Wrap each tuna filet in two slices of lard. Steam for about 5 minutes in a steamer basket set over boiling water. Meanwhile, season the melon with salt, pepper, and the lemon juice. Lightly fry the shallot in the olive oil, then add the port. Reduce the sauce in volume by half. Pour the balsamic vinegar and honey into a separate pan and also reduce in volume by half.

Place the tuna on the serving plate, cover it with the melon and drizzle over both sauces as decoration. If you wish, add a cherry tomato and a few baby spinach leaves as a garnish.

Fragole e ricotta

Strawberries and ricotta

Large, ruby-red strawberries arrive in Rome's fruit and vegetable markets from Terracima at the beginning of May and are sold until July. Their natural sweetness means they don't need much fiddling with, and you will find them served in trattorie either with a sprinkle of sugar and some lemon juice or with a more luscious dose of whipped cream. I find they also go very well with fresh sheep's milk ricotta, roughly mixed with chopped strawberries and some sugar that pulls out all the natural juices. It is a simple and rustic dessert, but it summarizes easy Roman dining – no fuss, just great ingredients.

13 oz ripe strawberries, halved
2 teaspoons sugar
1 tablespoon water
7 oz fresh ricotta
a few mint leaves

Place the strawberries in a large bowl. Sprinkle them with the sugar and then add the water. Gently mix and place in the refrigerator for 30 minutes to chill.

Serve the strawberries on individual dessert plates, with a scoop of ricotta cheese on top and a few mint leaves to garnish.

brac
ciano

Bracciano

The volcanic lakes around Rome, Bolsena, Albano, Bracciano, and Martignano are favorite day trips for the Romans escaping summer's sweltering city heat. Lake Bracciano's deep, breeze-swept waters make it a perfect location for windsurfing, kayaking, and sailing regattas, while the many natural reserves around it are ideal for walkers and birdwatchers. All along the lake, little restaurants on the lava-sand beaches serve up eels fried in golden batter and roasted trout to the day-trippers, who then take to their loungers for an afternoon siesta and a spot of sun-worshipping. However pleasurable the experience might be, it's quite difficult to find places serving lakeside fish in a palatable way. Blame it on the farming, which has reduced eel and trout to tasteless, fatty fish, and the lazy reliance on fast-food recipes – few are the places which treat this indigenous resource in an adventurous way.

An exception to the rule of bland gastronomy around the lake is Vino e Camino, a delightful *enoteca* in Bracciano. Easy to reach thanks to the high-speed train from the center of Rome, the enoteca is strategically placed in the town center in front of the majestic Orsini castle. The other two towns around the lake, Anguillara and Trevignano, are equally picturesque destinations, but my preference has always been at Vino e Camino. This is no doubt aided by the thought of a delicious lunch stop at one of their outdoor tables under the cooling shade of an umbrella and with a view of the castle.

Siblings Cristina and Massimo Baroni have enthusiastically rethought Roman cuisine and conjured up a formula that has everyone coming back for more. While Cristina effortlessly adapts traditional dishes, with an awareness of her culinary heritage as well as a healthy dose of irreverence, Massimo has built up a formidable selection of wines, with the focus on small producers and reasonable prices. Massimo's wife, Paola, "lends" a hand rustling up delicious pastries and spreading her polyglot charm to customers – all this when she is not tending to her four young children. Her natural curiosity about the history of Bracciano means that the restaurant has become the place to go to taste products still painstakingly made in the traditional way. Thanks to Paola's patronage, Sisto Mercantina and wife Clara Canini's butchery is featured in Italian food guides, their handmade pork liver sausages hailed as a triumph of taste. But it's the delicate fennel-seasoned smoked *porchetta* that has earnt them a place in meat-lovers' hearts. The porchetta is slowly roasted for about 8 hours under a sheet of wax paper in Bracciano's oldest oven, active since 1200.

Opposite: The Orsini castle in Bracciano is the perfect setting for an alfresco lunch at top enoteca Vino e Camino.

Food lovers' address book

Vino e Camino (restaurant)
Piazza Mazzini 11
Bracciano
tel +39 06 99803433

Norcineria La Moretta
(specialist sausage store)
Via Palazzi 4
Bracciano
tel +39 06 99804938

Involtini di luccio
Pike rolls

Luccio is pike, a fish commonly found in the lakes of Rome. For this recipe you can use any type of saltwater white fish, such as sea bass or cod.

6 large Cos (romaine) lettuce leaves
4 pike filets, about 15 oz
a little olive oil
1 garlic clove, chopped
scant 1/2 cup dry white wine
a few chives, chopped, plus a few left whole
1 egg, beaten
1 tablespoon dry breadcrumbs
wild rice to serve (optional)

Blanch the lettuce leaves in boiling salted water, then put the leaves in a bowl of water and ice to keep them green. Meanwhile pan-fry the filets with a little bit of olive oil and the garlic. Pour in the wine and a few chives. Cook until the wine has evaporated.

Remove the filets and dip into a bowl of beaten egg. Then cover both sides of the filet with breadcrumbs. Roll each one inside a lettuce leaf; the parcel can be tied together with a chive. Alternatively, place a bed of lettuce leaves on a baking tray, place the filets on it in a single layer and cover with some more lettuce leaves.

Bake in a preheated oven at 325°F for 10 minutes. The parcels can be served as a main dish accompanied by some wild rice.

Gazpacho di farro

Spelt gazpacho

Farro (spelt) is a type of hulled wheat widely used since ancient Roman times. Today farro is grown in the Garfagnana region of Tuscany, as well as in Lazio and Abbruzzi. Although it has always formed the basis of peasant-style soups, farro has enjoyed a culinary renaissance over the past years, perhaps aided by its reputation of boosting male fertility. Shops such as Volpetti in the Testacchio (see page 93) substitute rice with farro for their *arancini*, and even make a farro cake which is reminiscent of *la pastiera napoletana*, the traditional Neapolitan Easter cake. This recipe is Cristina's take on the traditional farro soup, a cool chilled gazpacho perfect for hot summer lunches. She uses *farricello*, broken spelt, which is quicker to cook.

10 oz farricello (broken spelt) or farro
4 vine-ripened tomatoes
1 red pepper
1 yellow pepper
1 cucumber, sliced
1 onion. sliced
a few basil leaves
olive oil
salt and freshly ground black peppor

Pour the farricello into a pot of boiling salted water. When tender, drain and set aside to cool. Meanwhile, place the tomatoes in a bowl and cover with boiling water. Leave for 1–2 minutes, then drain. Cut a cross at the stem end and peel off the skins. Pass through a sieve to get rid of the seeds.

Roast the peppers in a preheated oven at 400°F until the skins blacken. Remove from the oven, place in a saucepan and cover. When cool, the skins should peel off easily.

Purée the tomato, peppers, cucumber, and onion in a food processor or liquidizer until smooth. In a bowl, mix the purée with the farro and chill for at least a couple of hours. Serve directly from the refrigerator with a few basil leaves as a garnish, some freshly ground black pepper, and some drizzled olive oil.

Ricotta al forno con fiori di zucchina

Oven-baked ricotta with zucchini flowers

This is one of Cristina's simplest recipes, one that uses staple Roman ingredients such as ricotta cheese and zucchini flowers. Since I'm aware of the difficulties of finding zucchini flowers outside Italy – although some greengrocers and Italian delicatessens do stock them – I suggest substituting them with actual zucchini, although to achieve the same sweet taste one should aim for smallish, organic ones, the kind that have ripened in the sun. Or grow your own!

4 zucchini flowers or 3 zucchini, about 7 oz, sliced
1 coffeespoon anchovy paste
10 oz fresh ricotta

Gently fry the zucchini flowers (or the sliced zucchini) with the anchovy paste. When ready, mix with the ricotta. Pour the mixture into a deep baking dish and bake in a preheated oven at 325°F for about 30 minutes. Remove from the oven, cut into slices, and serve warm.

sper
longa

Sperlonga

Heading south, away from Rome and towards Naples, one reaches the tiny whitewashed fishing village of Sperlonga. This is a favorite retreat for many Romans who decamp to their seaside homes during the summer. The Emperor Tiberius chose Sperlonga for his impressive villa, partially created out of a grotto and full of marble statues celebrating Ulysses' heroic gestures. The remains of the villa, located at the end of the beach of Levante, can be visited, and still reveal the structures for thermal baths and a private port.

Sperlonga's name probably derives from the many grottoes found along this coastline, called *speluncae* in Latin, which used to be the homes of the local inhabitants, who then gradually settled on the hill of San Magno. The medieval part of the town, clinging precariously to the hill, is a suggestive warren of meandering narrow roads, arches, and small, cubed houses.

Sperlonga comes into its own during the summer, when the central *piazzetta* fills with sunbathers sipping their early evening cocktails and the tourists crowd the restaurants in the back streets, enjoying unfussy fresh fare. Nestled under an arch and down a series of steep steps is Gli Archi, one of the most renowned Sperlonga restaurants. Housed in a converted stable, in the summer it also enjoys an alfresco dining area perched on a raised terrace and under the shade of bougainvillea and palm trees. Owner Lino Farina rustles up simple dishes such as *spaghetti alle vongole*, *risotto alla crema di scampi*, and clam sauté, all made with the fresh daily catch that arrives in a fisherman's basket every evening.

The nearby plains are fertile lands blessed with some of the best Lazio produce. Large ripe artichokes come from Sezze, Catalan *puntarelle* (chicory) salad has been cultivated near Gaeta since ancient Roman times, as well as the tasty black olives that are bottled in *salamoia* (salted water) or used in savory cakes. But above all, this is the land of buffalo, which roam the plains of nearby Fondi and from the milk of which is produced a chewy, snow-white, melt-in-the-mouth type of mozzarella cheese, named after the Pontina area to distinguish it from the other types produced further south. The term "mozzarella" comes from the ancient tradition of *mozzare*, cutting the curd by hand, something that today is left to machines. The sweet-tasting white celery is another Sperlonga speciality, planted in the fields in the 1950s and now exported around the world. It is usually eaten as an ingredient of *pinzimonio*, a selection of raw carrots, celery, and tomatoes served with a vinaigrette. The Sperlonga restaurant Tramonto even makes a mouth-cleansing ice cream out of it.

Opposite: Sperlonga's faded charm attracts a mix of Roman and Neapolitan residents for the summer holidays. The area is known for its sweet buffalo mozzarella.

Food lovers' address book

Tramonto (restaurant)
Via Cristoforo Colombo 6/8
tel +39 0771 548932
Gli Archi (restaurant)
Via Ottaviano 17
tel +39 0771 548300
Caseificio Buoanno
(mozzarella producer)
Via Mole della Corti 7
Fondi
tel +39 0771 519026
Caseificio di Sarra Eugenio
(mozzarella producer)
Via Santa Anastasia 104
Fondi
tel +39 0771 555107

Spaghetti alle vongole
Spaghetti with clams

The quintessential summer dish, it only needs fresh clams to work wonders. Romans have always adored seafood, especially cockles, clams, mussels, and razor clams. There is something incredibly satisfying about digging the clams out of the shells and tossing them back into warm spaghetti. Every restaurant worth its salt around the Rome *litorale* – sea coast – will cook *spaghetti alle vongole*, often called *veraci* (authentic), as if to certify their freshness.

1 lb 12 oz unshelled clams
2 garlic cloves, chopped
**1 red chili, deseeded and finely chopped, or 1/2 teaspoon
  chili flakes**
a little olive oil
1 lb spaghetti
scant 1/2 cup dry white wine
1 teaspoon chopped flat-leaf parsley

Scrub the clam shells clean with a nailbrush and place them in a bucket of water for a couple of hours, then drain. Discard any open clams.
Fry the garlic and the chili in a frying pan or skillet with a little olive oil. Meanwhile cook the spaghetti in a large pot of boiling salted water. Pour the clams into the frying pan with the white wine and a little bit of water. Cover the pan with a lid and allow the clams to open up, sautéing slightly. As soon as they have opened, turn off the heat off and toss with the drained spaghetti in the pan with all the juices. Mix thoroughly, sprinkle with parsley, and serve immediately.

Pizza, prosciutto e fichi

Pizza, ham, and figs

This is a starter or a snack, served on hot summer days and perfect for beach picnics. The warm, salty pizza counterbalances the sweet flavor of the Parma ham and that of the mature, juicy figs.

10 oz cooked white pizza (see page 20)
3 1/2 oz or 4 thin slices of Parma ham
4 or 5 mature figs, sliced

Cut the pizza into four slices, then open them up with a serrated bread knife to make a pocket. Fill with the slices of Parma ham and figs.

La tiella di Gaeta

Gaeta savory pie

The cuisine of Rome and Lazio makes abundant use of savory pies. Romans usually eat them as a starter or appetizer, but they work equally well as a main dish with a fresh green salad. Black Gaeta olives, produced in the areas of Fondi and Gaeta, are the key ingredient.

For the pastry
2 1/4 cups Italian type 0 flour
pinch of salt
2 teaspoons sugar (this helps the yeast to rise)
2 dessertspoons olive oil
1/2 oz fresh yeast or 1 packet (1/4 oz) easy-blend dried yeast, dissolved in 1 tablespooon water
7/8 cup warm water

For the filling
3 1/2 oz pitted black Gaeta olives
14 oz fresh anchovy filets, finely chopped
2 medium vine-ripened tomatoes, cut into chunks
1 garlic clove, finely chopped
1 small red chili, deseeded and finely chopped, or 1 teaspoon chili flakes
a few flat-leaf parsley leaves, chopped
3 dessertspoons olive oil

To make the pastry, pour the flour into a bowl, make a hollow in the center and add the salt, sugar, olive oil, and yeast. Mix well, and slowly add the warm water. Knead for 10 minutes, then set it aside in a warm, dark place for 40–50 minutes or until doubled in volume.

Cut the pastry into two pieces, and roll out the first piece until it is large enough to cover the bottom and sides of a greased 10-inch diameter baking tin.

Place the olives, anchovies, and tomatoes on the pastry base with the garlic, chili, and parsley and drizzle with the olive oil.

Roll out the remaining dough and cover the filling, pressing the two pastry edges together. Prick the top with a fork and bake in a preheated oven at 400°F for about 30 minutes until the top is golden.

vino
veritas

Vino Veritas

With all the rich history surrounding the wines around Rome, it is a wonder that Lazio's stature as a wine-growing region is overshadowed these days by other, less historical areas. Lazio's wines have traditionally always been produced for the consumption of the inhabitants of Rome, and it is said that there is no place finer to make wine in the whole of Italy than upon the slopes and volcanic hills of this region. It is the wine that is drunk in Rome's cafés, bars, and restaurants and has a quality of quiet restraint which is preferred by the Romans themselves. It is no surprise that the region's production is dominated by white wines for drinking, usually with food or as an *aperitivo* on balmy summer evenings. Local wine has never been fussed over in Rome, and the wines reflect that. There is, however, a subtlety that hides the evidence of the gradual improvement in quality and stature. Lazio's best-kept secret is that the area around Frascati, which was often the source of fodder for the supermarket bottom shelf, is once again producing fabulous wines. Impressively, a small group of determined producers are creating magnificent red wines that are fast becoming the bargains of the increasingly pricey Italian wine scene.

The history of wine in Italy can claim its origins in Rome, where the cultivation of grapevines can be traced back to Romulus and Remus themselves. The Ancient Romans, impressed by the import of Greek winemaking, decided to develop similar skills on the slopes around the city. As the Roman Empire grew, so did the laying down of vineyards across its expanse. Every Roman drank wine as a daily routine, so swathes of vineyards were created around the outskirts of Rome to supply the demand. By AD 51 so many vines had been planted that Emperor Domitian forbade the planting of new vines to allow some of the land to be used for growing crops instead.

The Romans soon developed a high culture for their wines. According to Pliny the Elder, the Falernian wine, prized above all others, was aged for 25 years or more, and the vines were trained to grow up the trunks of elm trees. After the Empire disintegrated, wine production diminished, only to establish itself again in medieval times. An oft-recounted story tells that a bishop's servant in the twelfth century, tasting wines for his master, was so smitten with the wine that he tripled the mark "!" usually prescribed for the very best. This was how the white wine Est! Est!! Est!!! from the northern corner of Lazio got its name.

Opposite: Corks at Ferrara Enoteca; page 151, Lazio producers Casale Del Giglio and Casal de Paolis are some of the region's rising stars; page 153, the vineyards of Casal de Paolis near Frascati.

Lazio's more recent history has been a mixed blessing. In the 1960s and 1970s, wine production was dictated by the trend towards quantity. Producers influenced by national agricultural drives planted grape varieties for their high yields, at the cost of personality and flavor. Lazio produced bland wines in bulk. As demand changed and consumption steered itself on to quality, things have improved. Lazio producers have noted the success of neighboring regions which have reintroduced quality with better grape varieties, careful maintenance of their vines, and modern fermentation techniques.

Today a group of determined producers are re-establishing quality and reviving the region's reputation beyond that of those happy to retain the bulk-production status quo. These producers are reviving the qualities found in indigenous grape varieties grown only in Italy, edging out the bland Trebbiano grape and focusing on Malvasia di Candida, Greco, Bonvino, Cacchione, and Bombino Bianco. More adventurous white-wine producers are experimenting with the imported varieties of Sauvignon, Chardonnay, and Voigner, while others are turning to classic red varieties to make internationally accepted wines such as Merlot, Cabernet, Syrah, and Petit Verdot. You can also find Italian varieties such as Sangiovese, Monteulciano, Nero Buono, and Cesanese.

The vineyards of Lazio that feed the thirsty Romans are scattered about the far corners of the region, covering a distance of more than 140 miles from north to south. At the northern corner, bordering Umbria and Tuscany, are the vineyards situated around Lake Bolzena. The area is well known for Est! Est!! Est!!!, while many of the best reds of Lazio are made around the town of Montefiascone. There is also a small enclave of Orvieto production on the Lazio side of the border. Further south is another zone along the stretch of coast that goes from Civitavecchia to the town of Cerveteri. Although this is also where a lot of the bulk-produced reds and whites are made, in between there is a scattering of good producers. Further south, past Rome itself, the suburbs give way to the slow climb up to the town of Frascati, culminating at the volcanic peaks of the Castelli Romani and the Colli Albani. The great white-wine producers of Rome call this home; their vineyards sit in the best positions above the vineyards geared for mass production that supply the world with cheap Frascati. The best vineyards are situated around the towns of Marino, Grottaferrata, and Frascati itself. A 15-minute drive south, over the Colli Albani, are the vineyards of Velletri, Aprilia, and Cori. Here the white wines compete for quality with the better known whites of Frascati. West of the Castelli, the area rises into the unmistakable arid but beautiful hills that stretch all the way down to Naples. Here, in the area around Anagni and Piglio, is where up-and-coming producers are making quality reds under the Cesanese del Piglio DOC label. Further south past Frosinone and Latina are the vineyards in the hills that continue down to Casino. The small enclave around the coastal town of Terracina produces a good Moscato di Terracina Passito.

Sitting in a good *enoteca* on the streets of Rome or in the restaurants and stores in Frascati offering *degustazione dei vini* (wine tastings) is where a wide spectrum of wines from this region is available. Quality red wines can now be widely sampled. There are, for instance, the wines of Riccardo Cotarella's Falesco label in Montifiascone. All Falesco's red wines are spicy, intense, and well balanced, as well as being great value for

money, but it is his single vineyard, Montiano, that has cemented Cotarella's reputation as one of the finest producers of Merlot in Italy. In the Castelli Romani, Giullio and Fabrizio Santarelli produce their excellent Quattro Mori under the Castel de Paolis label. Across from the beautiful Castel de Paolis vineyards in Grottaferrata is the base of Colle Picchione in neighboring Marino, where 80-year-old producer Paola Di Mauro and her son Armando produce the blackcurrant and licorice red Vigna del Vassallo. In Aprilia, Casal del Giglio produces plummy Petit Verdots and ruby-colored Merlots. Further west in the region by Agnani can be found the well-known reds of Colacicchi and, in neighboring Piglio, a group of producers is raising the standard of the red wine Cesanese del Piglio. Those trying to establish quality are Terre Del Cesanese, Massimo Berucci, and the Cantina Sociale Cesanese del Piglio.

Lazio is famous for its whites. In Montifiascone, both Falesco and Paolo and Roberto Trappolini are producing Est! Est!! Est!!! with a surprising quality that belies its reputation. Neighbors Paolo and Noemia d'Amico produce the straw-and-yellow-tinged Falesia from their estate in Viano. Along the Coast at Civitella, Sergio Mottura produces complex whites and rich dessert wines from the indigenous Grechetto grape. In Frascati and the Castelli Romani, there is an abundance of independent producers delivering quality. Conte Zandotti produces a Malvasia del Lazio that establishes how much character these Italian grapes can produce. Villa Simone, Castel de Paolis, and production giant Fontana Candida all produce quality Frascati Superior. Wine from Fontana Candida's single vineyard, Santa Teresa, is widely available in the United Kingdom. Castel de Paolis's Villa Adriana is a blend of Malvasia and Viognier, and is superb. One tradition of Frascati is to produce a Frascati Cannellino, a light sweet wine. You can also find sparkling wine from these hills. If you can root it out, expect it to be zippy and perfect for an aperitivo.

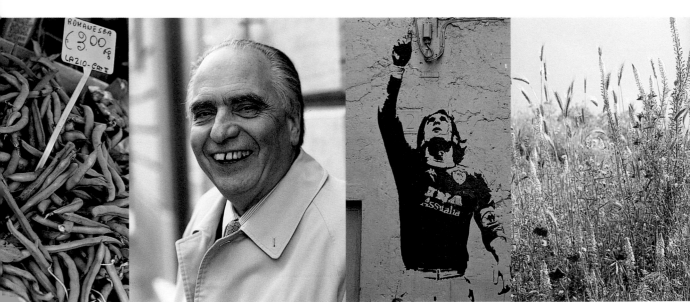

154

MOSCATO
ALEATICO
AMARO TON
FERRO - CH

DEGUST

155

Index

Page numbers in italic refer to the illustrations

Acknowledgments

A special thanks goes to my mother Felicity Williams for testing the recipes. This book is largely due to the love for food that she instilled in me as a child. Another thank you goes to my husband Neil Churcher for his patient proofreading and for sharing his knowledge about wines. Lisa Linder for her captivating photographs, her ability to convince everyone to pose for her and for being such a great companion on our trips. Katey Day for her guidance and patience. Lucy Gowans for her beautiful design. Michael Alcock for his encouragement and enthusiasm. Nadia Manuelli for continuing support. Massimo e Paola Baroni at Vino e Camino for their friendship, Cristina Baroni for her fabulous food. Wendy Artin for her suggestions and help, and for being with husband Bruno and daughter Lily, such great Roman company. John and Emily Benbow for testing recipes out while with a newborn baby and always cooking us great meals. Giulio Santarelli of Castel de Paolis for his warm and charming welcome. Agata Parisella at Agata e Romeo for recipes. Alberto Ciarla for his recipes and great storytelling. Salvatore Tassa for his hospitality and sharing his wonderful recipes. Signora Meloni at Tavola con lo Chef and all the school staff for their welcome and help. Adriana Montellanico e Alberto Lombardi at La Briciola for their warm hospitality, generosity, and recipes. Dino e Tony for their verve and Paolo Buttarini and his wife, my friend Annarita Cillis for sharing their favorite restaurant with me. Pierluigi and Alessandro Roscioli for their suggestions, help, and generosity. Paolo D'Alicandro chef at Roscioli for his good cooking and recipes. Elio e Francesco Mariani brothers at Checchino restaurant for their humor and recipes. Aldo Trabalzi at Sora Lella for his stories, availability, and recipes, Leopoldo and Paolo Cacciani at Cacciani for their hospitality and recipes. All the staff at Sora Margherita for recipes and anecdotes. Everyone at the Forno di Piazza Campo di Fiori for pizza. Marco Gallotta at Gusto and Osteria della Frezza and Doriana for their help and support and recipes. Fabio Baldassare and Belinda Bortolan at L'Altro di Mastai for their kindness, support, and recipes. Rosaria Mondello for her timely introduction to brothers Massimo and Federica Riccioli alla Rosetta. Massimo Riccioli for one of my best lunches ever. Gloria Gravina and chef Andrea Buscema at Uno e Bino for the recipes. Chef Antonio Chiappini at Rosario restaurant in Ostia for the recipes. Lino Farina at the Archi restaurant for the hospitality.